Schöningh
westermann

AF635701

EinFach
Englisch

Oscar Wilde

The Importance of Being Earnest

A Trivial Comedy for Serious People

Edited by
Till Kinzel and Bianca Schwindt

Series Editor:
Hans Kröger

Acknowledgements

Illustrations

|akg-images GmbH, Berlin: 60, 65; Francis Frith Coll. 65. |Alamy Stock Photo (RMB), Abingdon/Oxfordshire: Pictorial Press Ltd 62. |Fotofinder GmbH, Berlin: Still Pictures/Hays, Philippe 4. |Keystone Pressedienst, Hamburg: 62. |Picture-Alliance GmbH, Frankfurt a.M.: akg-images 64; dpa 4, 63; dpa/Thissen, Bernd 4; dpa/UPI 5; epa/AFP/Maury 5; epa/Reynolds, Michael 4; KPA/TopFoto 62; united archives/WHA 62. |Presse- und Informationsamt der Bundesregierung, Berlin: 5. |Shutterstock.com, New York: Uncle Leo 4. |ullstein bild, Berlin: AP 5; heritage 64.

Sprachliche Betreuung: Simone Duxbury-Ziemer

Georg-Westermann-Allee 66, 38104 Braunschweig
www.westermann.de

Druck A^{6} / Jahr 2023
Alle Drucke der Serie A sind im Unterricht parallel verwendbar.

Umschlaggestaltung: Jennifer Kirchhof
Umschlagabbildung: Alamy Stock Photo/GRANGER - Historical Picture Archive
Druck und Bindung: Westermann Druck Zwickau GmbH, Crimmitschauer Str. 43, 08058 Zwickau

ISBN 978-3-14-**041196**-7

Contents

Getting started

1. What was/is essential to these persons?
2. What are important aims in your life?
3. Speculate on the meaning of the title *The Importance of Being Earnest.*

To
Robert Baldwin Ross
In Appreciation
In Affection

The Persons of the Play

JOHN WORTHING, J.P., of the Manor House, Woolton, Hertfordshire
ALGERNON MONCRIEFF, his friend
REV. CANON CHASUBLE, D.D., Rector of Woolton
MERRIMAN, butler to Mr. Worthing
LANE, Mr. Moncrieff's manservant
LADY BRACKNELL
HON. GWENDOLEN FAIRFAX, her daughter
CECILY CARDEW, John Worthing's ward
MISS PRISM, her governess

J. P. Justice of the Peace; a local judicial official empowered to perform minor legal tasks such as marriage ceremonies, certifying documents, etc.; usually highly respected in the community
Manor House the main house on an estate (= a large piece of land)
Rev. Reverend; a member of the clergy, a pastor/priest
D. D. Doctor of Divinity; *Doktor der Theologie*
Rector the head of a school or a religious institution
ward a person who is protected or looked after by sb else
governess a female teacher, esp. in a private household
Half-Moon Street Street in the fashionable West End of London

The Scenes of the Play

Act I *Algernon Moncrieff's Flat in Half-Moon Street, W.*
Act II *The Garden at the Manor House, Woolton*
Act III *Morning-Room at the Manor House, Woolton*

Time: The Present

The Importance of Being Earnest

Act I

Scene – Morning-room in ALGERNON'S *flat in Half-Moon Street. The room is luxuriously and artistically furnished. The sound of a piano is heard in the adjoining room.*

(LANE is *arranging afternoon tea on the table, and after the music has ceased,* ALGERNON *enters.*)

ALGERNON: Did you hear what I was playing, Lane?

LANE: I didn't think it polite to listen, sir.

ALGERNON: I'm sorry for that, for your sake. I don't play accurately – any one can play accurately – but I play with wonderful expression. As far as the piano is concerned, sentiment is my forte. I keep science for Life.

LANE: Yes, sir.

ALGERNON: And, speaking of the science of Life, have you got the cucumber sandwiches cut for Lady Bracknell?

LANE: Yes, sir. *(Hands them on a salver.)*

ALGERNON: *(Inspects them, takes two, and sits down on the sofa.)* Oh! ... by the way, Lane, I see from your book that on Thursday night, when Lord Shoreman and Mr. Worthing were dining with me, eight bottles of champagne are entered as having been consumed.

LANE: Yes, sir; eight bottles and a pint.

ALGERNON: Why is it that at a bachelor's establishment the servants invariably drink the champagne? I ask merely for information.

LANE: I attribute it to the superior quality of the wine, sir. I have often observed that in married households the champagne is rarely of a first-rate brand.

ALGERNON: Good heavens! Is marriage so demoralizing as that?

LANE: I believe it *is* a very pleasant state, sir. I have had very little experience of it myself up to the present. I have only been married once. That was in consequence of a misunderstanding between myself and a young person.

artistical showing skill in art
art
artist

sentiment here: emotional feelings
forte sb's strong point

salver a flat serving tray for presenting sandwiches, drinks, letters, etc.

bachelor an unmarried man
establishment household
invariably without exception

demoralizing weakening the spirit of sb

languidly *gelangweilt*

ALGERNON: *(Languidly.)* I don't know that I am much interested in your family life, Lane.

LANE: No, sir; it is not a very interesting subject. I never think of it myself.

ALGERNON: Very natural, I am sure. That will do, Lane, thank you.

LANE: Thank you, sir. *(LANE goes out.)*

lax loose, immoral

lower orders the lower classes of English society

ALGERNON: Lane's views on marriage seem somewhat lax. Really, if the lower orders don't set us a good example, what on earth is the use of them? They seem, as a class, to have absolutely no sense of moral responsibility.

(*Enter* LANE.)

LANE: Mr. Ernest Worthing.

(*Enter* JACK.)

(LANE *goes out.*)

ALGERNON: How are you, my dear Ernest? What brings you up to town?

JACK: Oh, pleasure, pleasure! What else should bring one anywhere? Eating as usual, I see, Algy!

customary common or expected practice

good society here: the fashionable and well-regarded people of the upper classes

ALGERNON: (*Stiffly.*) I believe it is customary in good society to take some slight refreshment at five o'clock. Where have you been since last Thursday?

JACK: (*Sitting down on the sofa.*) In the country.

ALGERNON: What on earth do you do there?

Characterize the relationship between Algernon and Jack.

JACK: (*Pulling off his gloves.*) When one is in town one amuses oneself. When one is in the country one amuses other people. It is excessively boring.

ALGERNON: And who are the people you amuse?

JACK: (*Airily.*) Oh, neighbours, neighbours.

Shropshire county in the centre of England, to the north-west of Birmingham

ALGERNON: Got nice neighbours in your part of Shropshire?

JACK: Perfectly horrid! Never speak to one of them.

ALGERNON: How immensely you must amuse them! (*Goes over and takes sandwich.*) By the way, Shropshire is your county, is it not?

reckless wild and careless (e.g. behaviour, spending, etc.)

extravagance careless spending of (a lot of) money

JACK: Eh? Shropshire? Yes, of course. Hallo! Why all these cups? Why cucumber sandwiches? Why such reckless extravagance in one so young? Who is coming to tea?

ALGERNON: Oh! merely Aunt Augusta and Gwendolen.

JACK: How perfectly delightful!

ALGERNON: Yes, that is all very well; but I am afraid Aunt Augusta won't quite approve of your being here.

JACK: May I ask why?

ALGERNON: My dear fellow, the way you flirt with Gwendolen is perfectly disgraceful. It is almost as bad as the way Gwendolen flirts with you.

JACK: I am in love with Gwendolen. I have come up to town expressly to propose to her.

ALGERNON: I thought you had come up for pleasure? ... I call that business.

JACK: How utterly unromantic you are!

ALGERNON: I really don't see anything romantic in proposing. It is very romantic to be in love. But there is nothing romantic about a definite proposal. Why, one may be accepted. One usually is, I believe. Then the excitement is all over. The very essence of romance is uncertainty. If ever I get married, I'll certainly try to forget the fact.

JACK: I have no doubt about that, dear Algy. The Divorce Court was specially invented for people whose memories are so curiously constituted.

ALGERNON: Oh! there is no use speculating on that subject. Divorces are made in Heaven – (JACK *puts out his hand to take a sandwich.* ALGERNON *at once interferes.*) Please don't touch the cucumber sandwiches. They are ordered specially for Aunt Augusta. (*Takes one and eats it.*)

JACK: Well, you have been eating them all the time.

ALGERNON: That is quite a different matter. She is my aunt. (*Takes plate from below.*) Have some bread and butter. The bread and butter is for Gwendolen. Gwendolen is devoted to bread and butter.

JACK: (*Advancing to table and helping himself.*) And very good bread and butter it is too.

ALGERNON: Well, my dear fellow, you need not eat as if you were going to eat it all. You behave as if you were married to her already. You are not married to her already, and I don't think you ever will be.

JACK: Why on earth do you say that?

ALGERNON: Well, in the first place girls never marry the men they flirt with. Girls don't think it right.

JACK: Oh, that is nonsense!

ALGERNON: It isn't. It is a great truth. It accounts for the extraordinary number of bachelors that one sees all over the place. In the second place, I don't give my consent.

JACK: Your consent!

ALGERNON: My dear fellow, Gwendolen is my first cousin. And before I allow you to marry her, you will have to clear up the whole question of Cecily. (*Rings bell.*)

JACK: Cecily! What on earth do you mean? What do you mean, Algy, by Cecily! I don't know anyone of the name of Cecily.

[*Enter* LANE.]

to propose here: to make an offer of marriage
proposal a formal suggestion or plan
proposition a plan of action that is suggested

The Divorce Court *Gerichtshof für Ehescheidungen*

constituted arranged or set up in a particular way

consent permission

smoking-room a separate room which the men of a household used for smoking

frantic here: desperate

Scotland Yard the London police force, so named after its original headquarters at a place called Great Scotland Yard in London

hard up (slang) short of money

inscription special text that is inscribed, i.e. written, engraved or printed on sth

ungentlemanly not befitting the behavior of a gentleman
gentleman a man of good education and social position who has excellent manners
hard-and-fast rule a clear rule that can always be used

Tunbridge Wells a seaside holiday area in Kent, south-east of London
to be fond of to have a liking or love for sth or sb

ALGERNON: Bring me that cigarette case Mr. Worthing left in the smoking-room the last time he dined here.

LANE: Yes, sir. (LANE *goes out.*)

JACK: Do you mean to say you have had my cigarette case all this time? I wish to goodness you had let me know. I have been writing frantic letters to Scotland Yard about it. I was very nearly offering a large reward.

ALGERNON: Well, I wish you would offer one. I happen to be more than usually hard up.

JACK: There is no good offering a large reward now that the thing is found.

(*Enter* LANE *with the cigarette case on a salver.* ALGERNON *takes it at once.* LANE *goes out.*)

ALGERNON: I think that is rather mean of you, Ernest, I must say. (*Opens case and examines it.*) However, it makes no matter, for, now that I look at the inscription inside, I find that the thing isn't yours after all.

JACK: Of course it's mine. (*Moving to him.*) You have seen me with it a hundred times, and you have no right whatsoever to read what is written inside. It is a very ungentlemanly thing to read a private cigarette case.

ALGERNON: Oh! it is absurd to have a hard-and-fast rule about what one should read and what one shouldn't. More than half of modern culture depends on what one shouldn't read.

JACK: I am quite aware of the fact, and I don't propose to discuss modern culture. It isn't the sort of thing one should talk of in private. I simply want my cigarette case back.

ALGERNON: Yes; but this isn't your cigarette case. This cigarette case is a present from someone of the name of Cecily, and you said you didn't know anyone of that name.

JACK: Well, if you want to know, Cecily happens to be my aunt.

ALGERNON: Your aunt!

JACK: Yes. Charming old lady she is, too. Lives at Tunbridge Wells. Just give it back to me, Algy.

ALGERNON: (*Retreating to back of sofa.*) But why does she call herself little Cecily if she is your aunt and lives at Tunbridge Wells? (*Reading.*) 'From little Cecily with her fondest love.'

JACK: (*Moving to sofa and kneeling upon it.*) My dear fellow, what on earth is there in that? Some aunts are tall, some aunts are not tall. That is a matter that surely an aunt may be allowed to decide for herself. You seem to think that every aunt should be exactly like your aunt! That is absurd! For Heaven's sake give me back my cigarette case. (*Follows* ALGERNON *round the room.*)

ALGERNON: Yes. But why does your aunt call you her uncle?

'From little Cecily, with her fondest love to her dear Uncle Jack.' There is no objection, I admit, to an aunt being a small aunt, but why an aunt, no matter what her size may be, should call her own nephew her uncle, I can't quite make out. Besides, your name isn't Jack at all; it is Ernest.

JACK: It isn't Ernest; it's Jack.

ALGERNON: You have always told me it was Ernest. I have introduced you to every one as Ernest. You answer to the name of Ernest. You look as if your name was Ernest. You are the most earnest-looking person I ever saw in my life. It is perfectly absurd your saying that your name isn't Ernest. It's on your cards. Here is one of them. (*Taking it from case.*) 'Mr. Ernest Worthing, B. 4, The Albany.' I'll keep this as a proof that your name is Ernest if ever you attempt to deny it to me, or to Gwendolen, or to any one else. (*Puts the card in his pocket.*)

JACK: Well, my name is Ernest in town and Jack in the country, and the cigarette case was given to me in the country.

ALGERNON: Yes, but that does not account for the fact that your small Aunt Cecily, who lives at Tunbridge Wells, calls you her dear uncle. Come, old boy, you had much better have the thing out at once.

JACK: My dear Algy, you talk exactly as if you were a dentist. It is very vulgar to talk like a dentist when one isn't a dentist. It produces a false impression.

ALGERNON: Well, that is exactly what dentists always do. Now, go on! Tell me the whole thing. I may mention that I have always suspected you of being a confirmed and secret Bunburyist; and I am quite sure of it now.

JACK: Bunburyist? What on earth do you mean by a Bunburyist?

ALGERNON: I'll reveal to you the meaning of that incomparable expression as soon as you are kind enough to inform me why you are Ernest in town and Jack in the country.

JACK: Well, produce my cigarette case first.

ALGERNON: Here it is. (*Hands cigarette case.*) Now produce your explanation, and pray make it improbable. (*Sits on sofa.*)

JACK: My dear fellow, there is nothing improbable about my explanation at all. In fact it's perfectly ordinary. Old Mr. Thomas Cardew, who adopted me when I was a little boy, made me in his will guardian to his grand-daughter, Miss Cecily Cardew. Cecily, who addresses me as her uncle from motives of respect that you could not possibly appreciate, lives at my place in the country under the charge of her admirable governess, Miss Prism.

ALGERNON: Where is that place in the country, by the way?

objection a reason against sth
to object to sb/sth to say that you disagree with
objector person who objects

What Impression does the name Ernest make on you?

The Albany a fashionable apartment building in London housing mainly bachelors

Bunburyist term invented by Oscar Wilde to describe sb living a double life

improbable difficult to believe

guardian a person given legal responsibility for sb else and their property, esp. if they are too young or otherwise unable to care for themselves

candidly openly

high moral tone high moral standards
to conduce to lead towards, to contribute to

dreadful scrape a disagreeable or shocking situation

tedious tiring or boring

invaluable extremely useful
invalid sb who is too ill to care for themself

Willis's a very fashionable restaurant where Oscar Wilde also liked to dine

JACK: That is nothing to you, dear boy. You are not going to be invited ... I may tell you candidly that the place is not in Shropshire.

ALGERNON: I suspected that, my dear fellow! I have Bunburyed all over Shropshire on two separate occasions. Now, go on. Why are you Ernest in town and Jack in the country?

JACK: My dear Algy, I don't know whether you will be able to understand my real motives. You are hardly serious enough. When one is placed in the position of guardian, one has to adopt a very high moral tone on all subjects. It's one's duty to do so. And as a high moral tone can hardly be said to conduce very much to either one's health or one's happiness, in order to get up to town I have always pretended to have a younger brother of the name of Ernest, who lives in the Albany, and gets into the most dreadful scrapes. That, my dear Algy, is the whole truth pure and simple.

ALGERNON: The truth is rarely pure and never simple. Modern life would be very tedious if it were either, and modern literature a complete impossibility!

JACK: That wouldn't be at all a bad thing.

ALGERNON: Literary criticism is not your forte, my dear fellow. Don't try it. You should leave that to people who haven't been at a University. They do it so well in the daily papers. What you really are is a Bunburyist. I was quite right in saying you were a Bunburyist. You are one of the most advanced Bunburyists I know.

JACK: What on earth do you mean?

ALGERNON: You have invented a very useful younger brother called Ernest, in order that you may be able to come up to town as often as you like. I have invented an invaluable permanent invalid called Bunbury, in order that I may be able to go down into the country whenever I choose. Bunbury is perfectly invaluable. If it wasn't for Bunbury's extraordinary bad health, for instance, I wouldn't be able to dine with you at Willis's to-night, for I have been really engaged to Aunt Augusta for more than a week.

JACK: I haven't asked you to dine with me anywhere to-night.

ALGERNON: I know. You are absurdly careless about sending out invitations. It is very foolish of you. Nothing annoys people so much as not receiving invitations.

JACK: You had much better dine with your Aunt Augusta.

ALGERNON: I haven't the smallest intention of doing anything of the kind. To begin with, I dined there on Monday, and once a week is quite enough to dine with one's own relations. In the second place, whenever I do dine there I am always treated as a member of the family, and sent down with either no woman at all, or two. In the third place, I know perfectly well whom she will place me next to, to-night. She will place me next Mary Farquhar, who always flirts with her own husband across the dinner-table. That is not very pleasant. Indeed, it is not even decent ... and that sort of thing is enormously on the increase. The amount of women in London who flirt with their own husbands is perfectly scandalous. It looks so bad. It is simply washing one's clean linen in public. Besides, now that I know you to be a confirmed Bunburyist I naturally want to talk to you about Bunburying. I want to tell you the rules.

JACK: I'm not a Bunburyist at all. If Gwendolen accepts me, I am going to kill my brother, indeed I think I'll kill him in any case. Cecily is a little too much interested in him. It is rather a bore. So I am going to get rid of Ernest. And I strongly advise you to do the same with Mr. ... with your invalid friend who has the absurd name.

ALGERNON: Nothing will induce me to part with Bunbury, and if you ever get married, which seems to me extremely problematic, you will be very glad to know Bunbury. A man who marries without knowing Bunbury has a very tedious time of it.

JACK: That is nonsense. If I marry a charming girl like Gwendolen, and she is the only girl I ever saw in my life that I would marry, I certainly won't want to know Bunbury.

ALGERNON: Then your wife will. You don't seem to realise, that in married life three is company and two is none.

JACK: (*Sententiously.*) That, my dear young friend, is the theory that the corrupt French Drama has been propounding for the last fifty years.

ALGERNON: Yes; and that the happy English home has proved in half the time.

JACK: For heaven's sake, don't try to be cynical. It's perfectly easy to be cynical.

ALGERNON: My dear fellow, it isn't easy to be anything nowadays. There's such a lot of beastly competition about. (*The sound of an electric bell is heard.*) Ah! that must be Aunt Augusta. Only relatives, or creditors, ever ring in that Wagnerian manner. Now, if I get her out of the way for ten minutes, so that you can have an opportunity for proposing to Gwendolen, may I dine with you to-night at Willis's?

JACK: I suppose so, if you want to.

ALGERNON: Yes, but you must be serious about it. I hate people who are not serious about meals. It is so shallow of them.

to be sent down to have to sit with sb at dinner

to induce to make sb do sth, to persuade

Algernon: "A man who marries without knowing Bunbury has a very tedious time of it." Explain the quote and what it implies for his understanding of marriage.

sententiously full of seemingly wise remarks about morality or behaviour

propound to suggest sth, to promote

beastly here: strong and unfair

creditor a person that you owe money to

Wagnerian referring to the musical style of the German composer Richard Wagner (1813–1883), whose operas were regarded by some as rather loud and overdramatic

(*Enter* LANE.)

LANE: Lady Bracknell and Miss Fairfax.

(ALGERNON *goes forward to meet them. Enter* LADY BRACKNELL *and* GWENDOLEN.)

LADY BRACKNELL: Good afternoon, dear Algernon, I hope you are behaving very well.

ALGERNON: I'm feeling very well, Aunt Augusta.

LADY BRACKNELL: That's not quite the same thing. In fact the two things rarely go together. (*Sees* JACK *and bows to him with icy coldness*.)

ALGERNON: (*To* GWENDOLEN.) Dear me, you are smart!

GWENDOLEN: I am always smart! Am I not, Mr. Worthing?

JACK: You're quite perfect, Miss Fairfax.

GWENDOLEN: Oh! I hope I am not that. It would leave no room for developments, and I intend to develop in many directions. (GWENDOLEN *and* JACK *sit down together in the corner*.)

LADY BRACKNELL: I'm sorry if we are a little late, Algernon, but I was obliged to call on dear Lady Harbury. I hadn't been there since her poor husband's death. I never saw a woman so altered; she looks quite twenty years younger. And now I'll have a cup of tea, and one of those nice cucumber sandwiches you promised me.

altered changed

ALGERNON: Certainly, Aunt Augusta. (*Goes over to tea-table*.)

LADY BRACKNELL: Won't you come and sit here, Gwendolen?

GWENDOLEN: Thanks, mamma, I'm quite comfortable where I am.

ALGERNON: (*Picking up empty plate in horror*.) Good heavens! Lane! Why are there no cucumber sandwiches? I ordered them specially.

LANE: (*Gravely*.) There were no cucumbers in the market this morning, sir. I went down twice.

grave serious

ALGERNON: No cucumbers!

LANE: No, sir. Not even for ready money.

ready money cash (here implying that usually things would have been bought on credit)

ALGERNON: That will do, Lane, thank you.

LANE: Thank you, sir. (*Goes out*.)

ALGERNON: I am greatly distressed, Aunt Augusta, about there being no cucumbers, not even for ready money.

distressed very upset or sorry

LADY BRACKNELL: It really makes no matter, Algernon. I had some crumpets with Lady Harbury, who seems to me to be living entirely for pleasure now.

crumpet a small, round soft kind of unsweetened bread

ALGERNON: I hear her hair has turned quite gold from grief.

grief extreme sadness, esp. due to the death of sb dear
grief-stricken
to grieve

LADY BRACKNELL: It certainly has changed its colour. From what cause I, of course, cannot say. (ALGERNON *crosses and hands tea*.) Thank you. I've quite a treat for you to-night, Alger-

treat sth special to enjoy

non. I am going to send you down with Mary Farquhar. She is such a nice woman, and so attentive to her husband. It's delightful to watch them.

ALGERNON: I am afraid, Aunt Augusta, I shall have to give up the pleasure of dining with you to-night after all.

LADY BRACKNELL: (*Frowning.*) I hope not, Algernon. It would put my table completely out. Your uncle would have to dine upstairs. Fortunately he is accustomed to that.

ALGERNON: It is a great bore, and I need hardly say, a terrible disappointment to me, but the fact is I have just had a telegram to say that my poor friend Bunbury is very ill again. (*Exchanges glances with* JACK.) They seem to think I should be with him.

LADY BRACKNELL: It is very strange. This Mr. Bunbury seems to suffer from curiously bad health.

ALGERNON: Yes; poor Bunbury is a dreadful invalid.

LADY BRACKNELL: Well, I must say, Algernon, that I think it is high time that Mr. Bunbury made up his mind whether he was going to live or to die. This shilly-shallying with the question is absurd. Nor do I in any way approve of the modern sympathy with invalids. I consider it morbid. Illness of any kind is hardly a thing to be encouraged in others. Health is the primary duty of life. I am always telling that to your poor uncle, but he never seems to take much notice ... as far as any improvement in his ailment goes. I should be much obliged if you would ask Mr. Bunbury, from me, to be kind enough not to have a relapse on Saturday, for I rely on you to arrange my music for me. It is my last reception, and one wants something that will encourage conversation, particularly at the end of the season when every one has practically said whatever they had to say, which, in most cases, was probably not much.

ALGERNON: I'll speak to Bunbury, Aunt Augusta, if he is still conscious, and I think I can promise you he'll be all right by Saturday. Of course the music is a great difficulty. You see, if one plays good music, people don't listen, and if one plays bad music people don't talk. But I'll run over the programme I've drawn out, if you will kindly come into the next room for a moment.

LADY BRACKNELL: Thank you, Algernon. It is very thoughtful of you. (*Rising, and following* ALGERNON.) I'm sure the programme will be delightful, after a few expurgations. French songs I cannot possibly allow. People always seem to think that they are improper, and either look shocked, which is vulgar, or laugh, which is worse. But German sounds a

to frown to look in a disapproving way

to be accustomed to sth to be used to sth

shilly-shallying taking too long to make a decision

morbid unhealthy, unwholesome

duty what one has to do

ailment illness

relapse falling back into a worse condition after getting better

to rely on sb to depend on sb

reception a social occasion such as a party

expurgation the act of removing improper or impure elements

improper not decent or appropriate

vulgar ordinary, not very educated
vulgarity
to vulgarize

thoroughly respectable language, and indeed, I believe is so. Gwendolen, you will accompany me.

GWENDOLEN: Certainly, mamma.

(LADY BRACKNELL *and* ALGERNON *go into the music-room,* GWENDOLEN *remains behind.*)

JACK: Charming day it has been, Miss Fairfax.

GWENDOLEN: Pray don't talk to me about the weather, Mr. Worthing. Whenever people talk to me about the weather, I always feel quite certain that they mean something else. And that makes me so nervous.

JACK: I do mean something else.

GWENDOLEN: I thought so. In fact, I am never wrong.

JACK: And I would like to be allowed to take advantage of Lady Bracknell's temporary absence ...

GWENDOLEN: I would certainly advise you to do so. Mamma has a way of coming back suddenly into a room that I have often had to speak to her about.

JACK: (*Nervously.*) Miss Fairfax, ever since I met you I have admired you more than any girl ... I have ever met since ... I met you.

GWENDOLEN: Yes, I am quite well aware of the fact. And I often wish that in public, at any rate, you had been more demonstrative. For me you have always had an irresistible fascination. Even before I met you I was far from indifferent to you. (JACK *looks at her in amazement.*) We live, as I hope you know, Mr. Worthing, in an age of ideals. The fact is constantly mentioned in the more expensive monthly magazines, and has reached the provincial pulpits, I am told; and my ideal has always been to love some one of the name of Ernest. There is something in that name that inspires absolute confidence. The moment Algernon first mentioned to me that he had a friend called Ernest, I knew I was destined to love you.

JACK: You really love me, Gwendolen?

GWENDOLEN: Passionately!

JACK: Darling! You don't know how happy you've made me.

GWENDOLEN: My own Ernest!

JACK: But you don't really mean to say that you couldn't love me if my name wasn't Ernest?

GWENDOLEN: But your name is Ernest.

JACK: Yes, I know it is. But supposing it was something else? Do you mean to say you couldn't love me then?

GWENDOLEN: (*Glibly.*) Ah! that is clearly a metaphysical speculation, and like most metaphysical speculations has very little reference at all to the actual facts of real life, as we know them.

charming giving pleasure

temporary for a limited time

demonstrative showing an open expression of feelings, e.g. love
irresistible overpowering
indifferent not caring one way or the other
amazement state of complete wonder or astonishment
provincial belonging to the provinces, as opposed to the city (e.g. London)
pulpit a platform in a church from which a preacher gives a sermon
to inspire to breathe life into sth
confidence here: trust in sb
destined fated

glibly fluently, smoothly
metaphysical here: extremely abstract, theoretical

JACK: Personally, darling, to speak quite candidly, I don't much care about the name of Ernest ... I don't think the name suits me at all.

GWENDOLEN: It suits you perfectly. It is a divine name. It has a music of its own. It produces vibrations.

JACK: Well, really, Gwendolen, I must say that I think there are lots of other much nicer names. I think Jack, for instance, a charming name.

GWENDOLEN: Jack? ... No, there is very little music in the name Jack, if any at all, indeed. It does not thrill. It produces absolutely no vibrations. ... I have known several Jacks, and they all, without exception, were more than usually plain. Besides, Jack is a notorious domesticity for John! And I pity any woman who is married to a man called John. She would probably never be allowed to know the entrancing pleasure of a single moment's solitude. The only really safe name is Ernest.

JACK: Gwendolen, I must get christened at once – I mean we must get married at once. There is no time to be lost.

GWENDOLEN: Married, Mr. Worthing?

JACK: (*Astounded.*) Well ... surely. You know that I love you, and you led me to believe, Miss Fairfax, that you were not absolutely indifferent to me.

GWENDOLEN: I adore you. But you haven't proposed to me yet. Nothing has been said at all about marriage. The subject has not even been touched on.

JACK: Well ... may I propose to you now?

GWENDOLEN: I think it would be an admirable opportunity. And to spare you any possible disappointment, Mr. Worthing, I think it only fair to tell you quite frankly beforehand that I am fully determined to accept you.

JACK: Gwendolen!

GWENDOLEN: Yes, Mr. Worthing, what have you got to say to me?

JACK: You know what I have got to say to you.

GWENDOLEN: Yes, but you don't say it.

JACK: Gwendolen, will you marry me? (*Goes on his knees.*)

GWENDOLEN: Of course I will, darling. How long you have been about it! I am afraid you have had very little experience in how to propose.

JACK: My own one, I have never loved any one in the world but you.

GWENDOLEN: Yes, but men often propose for practice. I know my brother Gerald does. All my girl-friends tell me so. What wonderfully blue eyes you have, Ernest! They are quite, quite blue.

to suit to fit

divine godlike, heavenly

vibration here: a distinct emotional aura that is felt instinctively

to thrill to cause a sudden pleasant shudder

plain common, ordinary

domesticity here: a name only used among the family

entrancing delightful

solitude the state of being alone

to get christened *getauft werden*

astounded astonished, surprised

disappointment unhappiness or frustration due to the failure of one's hopes or expectations

before-hand before sth else happens

I hope you will always look at me just like that, especially when there are other people present. (*Enter* LADY BRACKNELL.)

semi-recumbent half lying down
posture way of holding the body
indecorous showing bad manners
retire here: to go back into another room
engaged *verlobt*

LADY BRACKNELL: Mr. Worthing! Rise, sir, from this semi-recumbent posture. It is most indecorous.

GWENDOLEN: Mamma! (*He tries to rise; she restrains him.*) I must beg you to retire. This is no place for you. Besides, Mr. Worthing has not quite finished yet.

LADY BRACKNELL: Finished what, may I ask?

GWENDOLEN: I am engaged to Mr. Worthing, mamma. (*They rise together.*)

Why is Lady Bracknell against Gwendolen's engagement to Jack?

LADY BRACKNELL: Pardon me, you are not engaged to anyone. When you do become engaged to someone, I, or your father, should his health permit him, will inform you of the fact. An engagement should come on a young girl as a surprise, pleasant or unpleasant, as the case may be. It is hardly a matter that she could be allowed to arrange for herself. ... And now I have a few questions to put to you, Mr. Worthing. While I am making these inquiries, you, Gwendolen, will wait for me below in the carriage.

carriage a horse-drawn cart
reproachful in a manner showing blame or disapproval of sth

GWENDOLEN: (*Reproachfully.*) Mamma!

LADY BRACKNELL: In the carriage, Gwendolen! (GWENDOLEN *goes to the door. She and* JACK *blow kisses to each other behind* LADY BRACKNELL'S *back.* LADY BRACKNELL *looks vaguely about as if she could not understand what the noise was. Finally turns round.*) Gwendolen, the carriage!

GWENDOLEN: Yes, mamma. (*Goes out, looking back at* JACK.)

Closely examine Lady Bracknell's interview with Jack. Characterize both of them.

LADY BRACKNELL: (*Sitting down.*) You can take a seat, Mr. Worthing.

(*Looks in her pocket for note-book and pencil.*)

JACK: Thank you, Lady Bracknell, I prefer standing.

eligible worthy of being chosen as a husband

LADY BRACKNELL: (*Pencil and note-book in hand.*) I feel bound to tell you that you are not down on my list of eligible young men, although I have the same list as the dear Duchess of Bolton has. We work together, in fact. However, I am quite ready to enter your name, should your answers be what a really affectionate mother requires. Do you smoke?

affectionate feeling or showing great love for sb

JACK: Well, yes, I must admit I smoke.

occupation here: activity, pastime

LADY BRACKNELL: I am glad to hear it. A man should always have an occupation of some kind. There are far too many idle men in London as it is. How old are you?

JACK: Twenty-nine.

LADY BRACKNELL: A very good age to be married at. I have always been of opinion that a man who desires to get married should know either everything or nothing. Which do you know?

JACK: (*After some hesitation.*) I know nothing, Lady Bracknell.

LADY BRACKNELL: I am pleased to hear it. I do not approve of anything that tampers with natural ignorance. Ignorance is like a delicate exotic fruit; touch it and the bloom is gone. The whole theory of modern education is radically unsound. Fortunately in England, at any rate, education produces no effect whatsoever. If it did, it would prove a serious danger to the upper classes, and probably lead to acts of violence in Grosvenor Square. What is your income?

JACK: Between seven and eight thousand a year.

LADY BRACKNELL: (*Makes a note in her book.*) In land, or in investments?

JACK: In investments, chiefly.

LADY BRACKNELL: That is satisfactory. What between the duties expected of one during one's lifetime, and the duties exacted from one after one's death, land has ceased to be either a profit or a pleasure. It gives one position, and prevents one from keeping it up. That's all that can be said about land.

JACK: I have a country house with some land, of course, attached to it, about fifteen hundred acres, I believe; but I don't depend on that for my real income. In fact, as far as I can make out, the poachers are the only people who make anything out of it.

LADY BRACKNELL: A country house! How many bedrooms? Well, that point can be cleared up afterwards. You have a town house, I hope? A girl with a simple, unspoiled nature, like Gwendolen, could hardly be expected to reside in the country.

JACK: Well, I own a house in Belgrave Square, but it is let by the year to Lady Bloxham. Of course, I can get it back whenever I like, at six months' notice.

LADY BRACKNELL: Lady Bloxham? I don't know her.

JACK: Oh, she goes about very little. She is a lady considerably advanced in years.

LADY BRACKNELL: Ah, nowadays that is no guarantee of respectability of character. What number in Belgrave Square?

JACK: 149.

LADY BRACKNELL: (*Shaking her head.*) The unfashionable side. I thought there was something. However, that could easily be altered.

JACK: Do you mean the fashion, or the side?

LADY BRACKNELL: (*Sternly.*) Both, if necessary, I presume. What are your politics?

JACK: Well, I am afraid I really have none. I am a Liberal Unionist.

hesitation waiting for a short period of time due to indecision or uncertainty
to hesitate
hesitant

to tamper with to change sth without being allowed to do so
unsound based on faulty ideas, incorrect
Grosvenor Square fashionable area in London's West End

duties taxes
to exact demand

attached to here: belonging to
acre a measure of land, approx. 4,047 square metres

poacher sb who steals wild animals by hunting them illegally

Belgrave Square a place in London's fashionable West End

six months' notice *sechsmonatige Kündigungsfrist*

to presume to suppose to be true

Liberal Unionist liberals who opposed Irish Home Rule at that time (1886)

Tory a member of the Conservative Party

purple of commerce those who became rich by selling and buying goods

charitable giving help to those in need, judging other people kindly
Worthing has been a seaside resort for the royal, the rich, and the fashionable from the eighteenth century on.
Sussex a county south of London
seaside resort a place at the coast where people go for holidays

cloak-room a place where coats and baggage can be left for a certain time
Victoria Station important train station in London on the southbound route
Brighton line the train line going from Victoria Station to Brighton on the south coast of England
immaterial of no importance
bewildered confused, puzzled
contempt a lack of respect
conceal to hide
social indiscretion behaviour or speech that does not follow the rules of society
assured solid, certain

LADY BRACKNELL: Oh, they count as Tories. They dine with us. Or come in the evening, at any rate. Now to minor matters. Are your parents living?

JACK: I have lost both my parents.

LADY BRACKNELL: To lose one parent, Mr. Worthing, may be regarded as a misfortune; to lose both looks like carelessness. Who was your father? He was evidently a man of some wealth. Was he born in what the Radical papers call the purple of commerce, or did he rise from the ranks of the aristocracy?

JACK: I am afraid I really don't know. The fact is, Lady Bracknell, I said I had lost my parents. It would be nearer the truth to say that my parents seem to have lost me ... I don't actually know who I am by birth. I was ... well, I was found.

LADY BRACKNELL: Found!

JACK: The late Mr. Thomas Cardew, an old gentleman of a very charitable and kindly disposition, found me, and gave me the name of Worthing, because he happened to have a first-class ticket for Worthing in his pocket at the time. Worthing is a place in Sussex. It is a seaside resort.

LADY BRACKNELL: Where did the charitable gentleman who had a first-class ticket for this seaside resort find you?

JACK: (*Gravely.*) In a hand-bag.

LADY BRACKNELL: A hand-bag?

JACK: (*Very seriously.*) Yes, Lady Bracknell. I was in a hand-bag – a somewhat large, black leather hand-bag, with handles to it – an ordinary hand-bag in fact.

LADY BRACKNELL: In what locality did this Mr. James, or Thomas, Cardew come across this ordinary hand-bag?

JACK: In the cloak-room at Victoria Station. It was given to him in mistake for his own.

LADY BRACKNELL: The cloak-room at Victoria Station?

JACK: Yes. The Brighton line.

LADY BRACKNELL: The line is immaterial. Mr. Worthing, I confess I feel somewhat bewildered by what you have just told me. To be born, or at any rate bred, in a hand-bag, whether it had handles or not, seems to me to display a contempt for the ordinary decencies of family life that reminds one of the worst excesses of the French Revolution. And I presume you know what that unfortunate movement led to? As for the particular locality in which the hand-bag was found, a cloak-room at a railway station might serve to conceal a social indiscretion – has probably, indeed, been used for that purpose before now – but it could hardly be regarded as an assured basis for a recognised position in good society.

JACK: May I ask you then what you would advise me to do? I need hardly say I would do anything in the world to ensure Gwendolen's happiness.

LADY BRACKNELL: I would strongly advise you, Mr. Worthing, to try and acquire some relations as soon as possible, and to make a definite effort to produce at any rate one parent, of either sex, before the season is quite over.

JACK: Well, I don't see how I could possibly manage to do that. I can produce the hand-bag at any moment. It is in my dressing-room at home. I really think that should satisfy you, Lady Bracknell.

LADY BRACKNELL: Me, sir! What has it to do with me? You can hardly imagine that I and Lord Bracknell would dream of allowing our only daughter – a girl brought up with the utmost care – to marry into a cloak-room, and form an alliance with a parcel? Good morning, Mr. Worthing!

(LADY BRACKNELL *sweeps out in majestic indignation.*)

JACK: Good morning! (ALGERNON, *from the other room, strikes up the Wedding March. Jack looks perfectly furious, and goes to the door.*) For goodness' sake don't play that ghastly tune, Algy. How idiotic you are!

(*The music stops and* ALGERNON *enters cheerily.*)

ALGERNON: Didn't it go off all right, old boy? You don't mean to say Gwendolen refused you? I know it is a way she has. She is always refusing people. I think it is most ill-natured of her.

JACK: Oh, Gwendolen is as right as a trivet. As far as she is concerned, we are engaged. Her mother is perfectly unbearable. Never met such a Gorgon … I don't really know what a Gorgon is like, but I am quite sure that Lady Bracknell is one. In any case, she is a monster, without being a myth, which is rather unfair … I beg your pardon, Algy, I suppose I shouldn't talk about your own aunt in that way before you.

ALGERNON: My dear boy, I love hearing my relations abused. It is the only thing that makes me put up with them at all. Relations are simply a tedious pack of people, who haven't got the remotest knowledge of how to live, nor the smallest instinct about when to die.

JACK: Oh, that is nonsense!

ALGERNON: It isn't!

JACK: Well, I won't argue about the matter. You always want to argue about things.

ALGERNON: That is exactly what things were originally made for.

JACK: Upon my word, if I thought that, I'd shoot myself …

to acquire to get, to obtain

alliance here: a connection between families

majestic very impressive
indignation anger that is caused by some injustice
furious very angry
ghastly horrible, shocking

as right as a trivet (coll.) perfectly o.k.

Gorgon in Greek mythology, a woman who has snakes growing on her head instead of hair and whose gaze turns people who look at her into stone; Gorgons were said to be very ugly

to abuse sb to say bad things about sb
tedious tiring, boring
remote here: slightest, tiniest bit

(*A pause.*) You don't think there is any chance of Gwendolen becoming like her mother in about a hundred and fifty years, do you, Algy?

ALGERNON: All women become like their mothers. That is their tragedy. No man does. That's his.

JACK: Is that clever?

ALGERNON: It is perfectly phrased! and quite as true as any observation in civilised life should be.

JACK: I am sick to death of cleverness. Everybody is clever nowadays. You can't go anywhere without meeting clever people. The thing has become an absolute public nuisance. I wish to goodness we had a few fools left.

nuisance sth annoying

ALGERNON: We have.

JACK: I should extremely like to meet them. What do they talk about?

ALGERNON: The fools? Oh! about the clever people, of course.

JACK: What fools!

ALGERNON: By the way, did you tell Gwendolen the truth about your being Ernest in town, and Jack in the country?

JACK: (*In a very patronising manner.*) My dear fellow, the truth isn't quite the sort of thing one tells to a nice, sweet, refined girl. What extraordinary ideas you have about the way to behave to a woman!

patronizing treating sb as if one were better or more important
refined having good taste or manners

ALGERNON: The only way to behave to a woman is to make love to her, if she is pretty, and to some one else, if she is plain.

plain unattractive

JACK: Oh, that is nonsense.

ALGERNON: What about your brother? What about the profligate Ernest?

profligate immoral, money-wasting, foolish

JACK: Oh, before the end of the week I shall have got rid of him. I'll say he died in Paris of apoplexy. Lots of people die of apoplexy, quite suddenly, don't they?

apoplexy the sudden loss of the ability to move or think etc. because of too much blood in the brain

ALGERNON: Yes, but it's hereditary, my dear fellow. It's a sort of thing that runs in families. You had much better say a severe chill.

JACK: You are sure a severe chill isn't hereditary, or anything of that kind?

hereditary sth that can be passed from one generation to another, esp. a disease or genetic defect

ALGERNON: Of course it isn't!

JACK: Very well, then. My poor brother Ernest is carried off suddenly, in Paris, by a severe chill. That gets rid of him.

to be carried off to die
severe very serious
chill a cold

ALGERNON: But I thought you said that ... Miss Cardew was a little too much interested in your poor brother Ernest? Won't she feel his loss a good deal?

JACK: Oh, that is all right. Cecily is not a silly romantic girl, I am glad to say. She has got a capital appetite, goes on long walks, and pays no attention at all to her lessons.

capital here: great, large

ALGERNON: I would rather like to see Cecily.

JACK: I will take very good care you never do. She is excessively pretty, and she is only just eighteen.

ALGERNON: Have you told Gwendolen yet that you have an excessively pretty ward who is only just eighteen?

JACK: Oh! one doesn't blurt these things out to people. Cecily and Gwendolen are perfectly certain to be extremely great friends. I'll bet you anything you like that half an hour after they have met, they will be calling each other sister.

to blurt sth out to say sth suddenly without thinking

ALGERNON: Women only do that when they have called each other a lot of other things first. Now, my dear boy, if we want to get a good table at Willis's, we really must go and dress. Do you know it is nearly seven?

JACK: (*Irritably.*) Oh! It always is nearly seven.

ALGERNON: Well, I'm hungry.

JACK: I never knew you when you weren't ...

ALGERNON: What shall we do after dinner? Go to a theatre?

JACK: Oh no! I loathe listening.

to loathe to hate strongly

ALGERNON: Well, let us go to the Club?

JACK: Oh, no! I hate talking.

ALGERNON: Well, we might trot round to the Empire at ten?

to trot round to go to a certain place
Empire the Holborn Empire, a music-hall in London

JACK: Oh, no! I can't bear looking at things. It is so silly.

ALGERNON: Well, what shall we do?

JACK: Nothing!

ALGERNON: It is awfully hard work doing nothing. However, I don't mind hard work where there is no definite object of any kind.

(*Enter* LANE.)

LANE: Miss Fairfax.

(*Enter* GWENDOLEN. LANE *goes out.*)

ALGERNON: Gwendolen, upon my word!

GWENDOLEN: Algy, kindly turn your back. I have something very particular to say to Mr. Worthing.

ALGERNON: Really, Gwendolen, I don't think I can allow this at all.

GWENDOLEN: Algy, you always adopt a strictly immoral attitude towards life. You are not quite old enough to do that.

(ALGERNON *retires to the fireplace.*)

JACK: My own darling!

GWENDOLEN: Ernest, we may never be married. From the expression on mamma's face I fear we never shall. Few parents nowadays pay any regard to what their children say to them. The old-fashioned respect for the young is fast dying out. Whatever influence I ever had over mamma, I lost at the age of three. But although she may prevent us from becoming man and wife, and I may marry some one else, and marry often, nothing that she can possibly do can alter my eternal devotion to you.

JACK: Dear Gwendolen!

GWENDOLEN: The story of your romantic origin, as related to me by mamma, with unpleasing comments, has naturally stirred the deeper fibres of my nature. Your Christian name has an irresistible fascination. The simplicity of your character makes you exquisitely incomprehensible to me. Your town address at the Albany I have. What is your address in the country?

JACK: The Manor House, Woolton, Hertfordshire.

(ALGERNON, *who has been carefully listening, smiles to himself, and writes the address on his shirt-cuff. Then picks up the Railway Guide.*)

GWENDOLEN: There is a good postal service, I suppose? It may be necessary to do something desperate. That of course will require serious consideration. I will communicate with you daily.

JACK: My own one!

GWENDOLEN: How long do you remain in town?

JACK: Till Monday.

GWENDOLEN: Good! Algy, you may turn round now.

ALGERNON: Thanks, I've turned round already.

GWENDOLEN: You may also ring the bell.

JACK: You will let me see you to your carriage, my own darling?

GWENDOLEN: Certainly.

JACK: (*To* LANE, *who now enters.*) I will see Miss Fairfax out.

LANE: Yes, sir. (JACK *and* GWENDOLEN *go off.*)

(LANE *presents several letters on a salver to* ALGERNON. *It is to be surmised that they are bills, as* ALGERNON, *after looking at the envelopes, tears them up.*)

ALGERNON: A glass of sherry, Lane.

LANE: Yes, sir.

ALGERNON: To-morrow, Lane, I'm going Bunburying.

LANE: Yes, sir.

ALGERNON: I shall probably not be back till Monday. You can put up my dress clothes, my smoking jacket, and all the Bunbury suits …

LANE: Yes, sir. (*Handing sherry.*)

ALGERNON: I hope to-morrow will be a fine day, Lane.

LANE: It never is, sir.

ALGERNON: Lane, you're a perfect pessimist.

LANE: I do my best to give satisfaction, sir.

devotion deep love or affection

fibres a person's inner character

incomprehensible impossible to understand

Hertfordshire is the childhood home of Queen Elizabeth I (Hatfield House).

shirt-cuff the end of a sleeve of a shirt

Railway Guide timetable for trains

to surmise to assume, to conclude

to put up to pack

dress clothes fine clothes worn in society

smoking jacket a jacket worn in the house to protect other clothes from tobacco smoke

(*Enter* Jack. Lane *goes off.*)

Jack: There's a sensible, intellectual girl! the only girl I ever cared for in my life. (Algernon *is laughing immoderately.*) What on earth are you so amused at?

Algernon: Oh, I'm a little anxious about poor Bunbury, that is all.

Jack: If you don't take care, your friend Bunbury will get you into a serious scrape some day.

Algernon: I love scrapes. They are the only things that are never serious.

Jack: Oh, that's nonsense, Algy. You never talk anything but nonsense.

Algernon: Nobody ever does.

(Jack *looks indignantly at him, and leaves the room.* Algernon *lights a cigarette, reads his shirt-cuff, and smiles.*)

ACT-DROP

immoderate beyond reasonable limits, excessive

act-drop end of this act

Act II

flight a continuous series of stairs
basket chair a chair woven out of thin pieces of wood
yew-tree *Eibe*
prism an object separating light into the colours of the rainbow
utilitarian practical, useful

Moulton Jack Worthing's gardener, who does not appear on the stage. He did so in the original four-act version of the play, which was later shortened to three acts by Oscar Wilde himself.

pray (formal) please
becoming fitting, pleasing, attractive

Analyse the moral and intellectual values of Miss Prism and their functions in the play.

to draw oneself up to stand up straight
gravity seriousness
demeanour outward behaviour towards others
to be commended to be praised

idle here: unproductive, unimportant
idleness not doing anything
idler
to idle away

merriment happiness and laughter
triviality unimportant things

Scene – Garden at the Manor House. A flight of grey stone steps leads up to the house. The garden, an old-fashioned one, full of roses. Time of year, July. Basket chairs, and a table covered with books, are set under a large yew-tree.

(MISS PRISM *discovered seated at the table.* CECILY *is at the back watering flowers.*)

MISS PRISM: (*Calling.*) Cecily, Cecily! Surely such a utilitarian occupation as the watering of flowers is rather Moulton's duty than yours? Especially at a moment when intellectual pleasures await you. Your German grammar is on the table. Pray open it at page fifteen. We will repeat yesterday's lesson.

CECILY: (*Coming over very slowly.*) But I don't like German. It isn't at all a becoming language. I know perfectly well that I look quite plain after my German lesson.

MISS PRISM: Child, you know how anxious your guardian is that you should improve yourself in every way. He laid particular stress on your German, as he was leaving for town yesterday. Indeed, he always lays stress on your German when he is leaving for town.

CECILY: Dear Uncle Jack is so very serious! Sometimes he is so serious that I think he cannot be quite well.

MISS PRISM: (*Drawing herself up.*) Your guardian enjoys the best of health, and his gravity of demeanour is especially to be commended in one so comparatively young as he is. I know no one who has a higher sense of duty and responsibility.

CECILY: I suppose that is why he often looks a little bored when we three are together.

MISS PRISM: Cecily! I am surprised at you. Mr. Worthing has many troubles in his life. Idle merriment and triviality would be out of place in his conversation. You must remember his constant anxiety about that unfortunate young man his brother.

CECILY: I wish Uncle Jack would allow that unfortunate young man, his brother, to come down here sometimes. We might have a good influence over him, Miss Prism. I am sure you certainly would. You know German, and geology, and things of that kind influence a man very much. (CECILY *begins to write in her diary.*)

MISS PRISM: (*Shaking her head.*) I do not think that even I could produce any effect on a character that according to his own brother's admission is irretrievably weak and vacillating. Indeed I am not sure that I would desire to reclaim him. I am not in favour of this modern mania for turning bad people into good people at a moment's notice. As a man sows so let him reap. You must put away your diary, Cecily. I really don't see why you should keep a diary at all.

CECILY: I keep a diary in order to enter the wonderful secrets of my life. If I didn't write them down, I should probably forget all about them.

MISS PRISM: Memory, my dear Cecily, is the diary that we all carry about with us.

CECILY: Yes, but it usually chronicles the things that have never happened, and couldn't possibly have happened. I believe that Memory is responsible for nearly all the three-volume novels that Mudie sends us.

MISS PRISM: Do not speak slightingly of the three-volume novel, Cecily. I wrote one myself in earlier days.

CECILY: Did you really, Miss Prism? How wonderfully clever you are! I hope it did not end happily? I don't like novels that end happily. They depress me so much.

MISS PRISM: The good ended happily, and the bad unhappily. That is what Fiction means.

CECILY: I suppose so. But it seems very unfair. And was your novel ever published?

MISS PRISM: Alas! no. The manuscript unfortunately was abandoned. I use the word in the sense of lost or mislaid. To your work, child, these speculations are profitless.

CECILY: (*Smiling.*) But I see dear Dr. Chasuble coming up through the garden.

MISS PRISM: (*Rising and advancing.*) Dr. Chasuble! This is indeed a pleasure.

(*Enter* CANON CHASUBLE.)

CHASUBLE: And how are we this morning? Miss Prism, you are, I trust, well?

CECILY: Miss Prism has just been complaining of a slight headache. I think it would do her so much good to have a short stroll with you in the Park, Dr. Chasuble.

MISS PRISM: Cecily, I have not mentioned anything about a headache.

CECILY: No, dear Miss Prism, I know that, but I felt instinctively that you had a headache. Indeed I was thinking about that, and not about my German lesson, when the Rector came in.

CHASUBLE: I hope, Cecily, you are not inattentive.

CECILY: Oh, I am afraid I am.

irretrievable (formal) sth that cannot be recovered or regained
vacillating changing from one opinion or emotion to another
to reclaim to make better in behaviour or character
mania desire for sth that is so strong as to appear mad

As a man sows so let him reap refers to a quote from the New Testament, Galatians 6:7

to chronicle to describe events in chronological order

Mudie the biggest lending library in London at the time
slighting showing a lack of respect for sth or sb

mislaid put in a place one cannot remember anymore
profitless for no good purpose or gain

Canon a Christian priest
Chasuble a long sleevless vestment worn by a priest when celebrating Mass

stroll a walk

Rector a priest in the Church of England who is in charge of a parish and also receives his income from there
inattentive unconcentrated, not paying attention

Chasuble: That is strange. Were I fortunate enough to be Miss Prism's pupil, I would hang upon her lips. (Miss Prism *glares.*) I spoke metaphorically. – My metaphor was drawn from bees. Ahem! Mr. Worthing, I suppose, has not returned from town yet?

Miss Prism: We do not expect him till Monday afternoon.

Chasuble: Ah yes, he usually likes to spend his Sunday in London. He is not one of those whose sole aim is enjoyment, as, by all accounts, that unfortunate young man his brother seems to be. But I must not disturb Egeria and her pupil any longer.

Miss Prism: Egeria? My name is Laetitia, Doctor.

Chasuble: (*Bowing.*) A classical allusion merely, drawn from the Pagan authors. I shall see you both no doubt at Evensong?

Miss Prism: I think, dear Doctor, I will have a stroll with you. I find I have a headache after all, and a walk might do it good.

Chasuble: With pleasure, Miss Prism, with pleasure. We might go as far as the schools and back.

Miss Prism: That would be delightful. Cecily, you will read your Political Economy in my absence. The chapter on the Fall of the Rupee you may omit. It is somewhat too sensational. Even these metallic problems have their melodramatic side.

(*Goes down the garden with* Dr. Chasuble.)

Cecily: (*Picks up books and throws them back on table.*) Horrid Political Economy! Horrid Geography! Horrid, horrid German!

(*Enter* Merriman *with a card on a salver.*)

Merriman: Mr. Ernest Worthing has just driven over from the station. He has brought his luggage with him.

Cecily: (*Takes the card and reads it.*) 'Mr. Ernest Worthing, B. 4, The Albany, W.' Uncle Jack's brother! Did you tell him Mr. Worthing was in town?

Merriman: Yes, Miss. He seemed very much disappointed. I mentioned that you and Miss Prism were in the garden. He said he was anxious to speak to you privately for a moment.

Cecily: Ask Mr. Ernest Worthing to come here. I suppose you had better talk to the housekeeper about a room for him.

Merriman: Yes, Miss.

(Merriman *goes off.*)

Cecily: I have never met any really wicked person before. I feel rather frightened. I am so afraid he will look just like everyone else.

(*Enter* Algernon, *very gay and debonair.*) He does!

Algernon: (*Raising his hat.*) You are my little cousin Cecily, I'm sure.

to glar to stare angrily

Egeria a Roman goddess who is the idealized model of a teacher

classical allusion a reference to sth from the ancient Greek and Roman eras

Pagan not Christian, i.e. Greek or Roman

Evensong evening religious service in the Church of England

Political Economy the study of how nations produce things and can get wealthy

Rupee unit of money used in India

sensational causing excited interest or attention

melodramatic showing or producing strong and excited feelings

horrid terrible or unpleasant

wicked morally bad

debonair cheerful and fashionably dressed

CECILY: You are under some strange mistake. I am not little. In fact, I believe I am more than usually tall for my age. (ALGERNON *is rather taken aback.*) But I am your cousin Cecily. You, I see from your card, are Uncle Jack's brother, my cousin Ernest, my wicked cousin Ernest.

ALGERNON: Oh! I am not really wicked at all, cousin Cecily. You mustn't think that I am wicked.

CECILY: If you are not, then you have certainly been deceiving us all in a very inexcusable manner. I hope you have not been leading a double life, pretending to be wicked and being really good all the time. That would be hypocrisy.

ALGERNON: (*Looks at her in amazement.*) Oh! Of course I have been rather reckless.

CECILY: I am glad to hear it.

ALGERNON: In fact, now you mention the subject, I have been very bad in my own small way.

CECILY: I don't think you should be so proud of that, though I am sure it must have been very pleasant.

ALGERNON: It is much pleasanter being here with you.

CECILY: I can't understand how you are here at all. Uncle Jack won't be back till Monday afternoon.

ALGERNON: That is a great disappointment. I am obliged to go up by the first train on Monday morning. I have a business appointment that I am anxious … to miss?

CECILY: Couldn't you miss it anywhere but in London?

ALGERNON: No, the appointment is in London.

CECILY: Well, I know, of course, how important it is not to keep a business engagement, if one wants to retain any sense of the beauty of life, but still I think you had better wait till Uncle Jack arrives. I know he wants to speak to you about your emigrating.

ALGERNON: About my what?

CECILY: Your emigrating. He has gone up to buy your outfit.

ALGERNON: I certainly wouldn't let Jack buy my outfit. He has no taste in neckties at all.

CECILY: I don't think you will require neckties. Uncle Jack is sending you to Australia.

ALGERNON: Australia! I'd sooner die.

CECILY: Well, he said at dinner on Wednesday night, that you would have to choose between this world, the next world, and Australia.

ALGERNON: Oh, well! The accounts I have received of Australia and the next world, are not particularly encouraging. This world is good enough for me, cousin Cecily.

CECILY: Yes, but are you good enough for it?

taken aback surprised in an unpleasant way

hypocrisy act of pretending to be different (mostly: better) than one is in reality
amazement astonishment
reckless wild and careless

to be obliged to have to do
obligation
obligatory

to retain to keep

to emigrate to move to another country and stay there permanently

necktie a narrow length of cloth worn around the neck and tied with a knot in front of the shirt

ALGERNON: I'm afraid I'm not that. That is why I want you to reform me. You might make that your mission, if you don't mind, cousin Cecily.

CECILY: I'm afraid I've no time, this afternoon.

ALGERNON: Well, would you mind my reforming myself this afternoon?

CECILY: It is rather Quixotic of you. But I think you should try.

ALGERNON: I will. I feel better already.

CECILY: You are looking a little worse.

ALGERNON: That is because I am hungry.

CECILY: How thoughtless of me. I should have remembered that when one is going to lead an entirely new life, one requires regular and wholesome meals. Won't you come in?

ALGERNON: Thank you. Might I have a buttonhole first? I never have any appetite unless I have a buttonhole first.

CECILY: A Maréchal Niel? (*Picks up scissors.*)

ALGERNON: No, I'd sooner have a pink rose.

CECILY: Why? (*Cuts a flower.*)

ALGERNON: Because you are like a pink rose, Cousin Cecily.

CECILY: I don't think it can be right for you to talk to me like that. Miss Prism never says such things to me.

ALGERNON: Then Miss Prism is a short-sighted old lady. (CECILY *puts the rose in his buttonhole.*) You are the prettiest girl I ever saw.

CECILY: Miss Prism says that all good looks are a snare.

ALGERNON: They are a snare that every sensible man would like to be caught in.

CECILY: Oh, I don't think I would care to catch a sensible man. I shouldn't know what to talk to him about.

(*They pass into the house.* MISS PRISM *and* DR. CHASUBLE *return.*)

MISS PRISM: You are too much alone, dear Dr. Chasuble. You should get married. A misanthrope I can understand – a womanthrope, never!

CHASUBLE: (*With a scholar's shudder.*) Believe me, I do not deserve so neologistic a phrase. The precept as well as the practice of the Primitive Church was distinctly against matrimony.

MISS PRISM: (*Sententiously.*) That is obviously the reason why the Primitive Church has not lasted up to the present day. And you do not seem to realise, dear Doctor, that by persistently remaining single, a man converts himself into a permanent public temptation. Men should be more careful; this very celibacy leads weaker vessels astray.

CHASUBLE: But is a man not equally attractive when married?

MISS PRISM: No married man is ever attractive except to his wife.

CHASUBLE: And often, I've been told, not even to her.

Quixotic referring to the literary figure Don Quixote in Cervantes' famous novel who fought against windmills, i.e. acted foolishly though with good intentions

wholesome healthy

buttonhole short form for flower worn in the buttonhole to decorate a man's jacket

Maréchal Niel a kind of rose with yellow flowers that was very popular in England after it was introduced in the 1860s

snare a trap for catching sth; sth by which one is trapped

misanthrope sb who hates human beings in general

womanthrope a new nonsense word created by Miss Prism, meaning a hater of woman, a misogynist

neologistic referring to a newly created word

precept rule for behaviour

Primitive Church the early Christian church, allegedly purer than in later times

matrimony state of being married

temptation sth that tempts, i.e. that makes one want to do sth considered wrong

celibacy the deliberate choice to stay unmarried and not have sexual relations

weaker vessels here: women without strong morals

astray into error or sin

MISS PRISM: That depends on the intellectual sympathies of the woman. Maturity can always be depended on. Ripeness can be trusted. Young women are green. (DR. CHASUBLE *starts.*) I spoke horticulturally. My metaphor was drawn from fruits. But where is Cecily?

CHASUBLE: Perhaps she followed us to the schools.

(*Enter* JACK *slowly from the back of the garden. He is dressed in the deepest mourning, with crape hatband and black gloves.*)

MISS PRISM: Mr. Worthing!

CHASUBLE: Mr. Worthing?

MISS PRISM: This is indeed a surprise. We did not look for you till Monday afternoon.

JACK: (*Shakes* MISS PRISM'S *hand in a tragic manner.*) I have returned sooner than I expected. Dr. Chasuble, I hope you are well?

CHASUBLE: Dear Mr. Worthing, I trust this garb of woe does not betoken some terrible calamity?

JACK: My brother.

MISS PRISM: More shameful debts and extravagance?

CHASUBLE: Still leading his life of pleasure?

JACK: (*Shaking his head.*) Dead!

CHASUBLE: Your brother Ernest dead?

JACK: Quite dead.

MISS PRISM: What a lesson for him! I trust he will profit by it.

CHASUBLE: Mr. Worthing, I offer you my sincere condolence. You have at least the consolation of knowing that you were always the most generous and forgiving of brothers.

JACK: Poor Ernest! He had many faults, but it is a sad, sad blow.

CHASUBLE: Very sad indeed. Were you with him at the end?

JACK: No. He died abroad; in Paris, in fact. I had a telegram last night from the manager of the Grand Hotel.

CHASUBLE: Was the cause of death mentioned?

JACK: A severe chill, it seems.

MISS PRISM: As a man sows, so shall he reap.

CHASUBLE: (*Raising his hand.*) Charity, dear Miss Prism, charity! None of us are perfect. I myself am peculiarly susceptible to draughts. Will the interment take place here?

JACK: No. He seems to have expressed a desire to be buried in Paris.

CHASUBLE: In Paris! (*Shakes his head.*) I fear that hardly points to any very serious state of mind at the last. You would no doubt wish me to make some slight allusion to this tragic domestic affliction next Sunday. (JACK *presses his hand convulsively.*) My sermon on the meaning of the

maturity ripeness, full development

horticultural referring to gardening

mourning here: black clothes showing one's grief for a person's death
crape black material worn as a sign of mourning

garb of woe clothes of mourning (as above)
to betoken (formal) to be a sign of
calamity a great misfortune

sincere condolence *aufrichtiges Beileid*
consolation sth that lessens the grief or sadness

charity here: show mercy and understanding
susceptible having little resistance
draught a current of air that often leads to a cold
interment burial
affliction suffering, unfortunate event
convulsive referring to violent and irregular muscular contractions

manna mentioned in the Bible (Exodus 16) as a substance miraculously provided as food for the Israelites in the wilderness
humiliation here: sadness, defeat
festal festive
Upper Orders higher classes of society

manna in the wilderness can be adapted to almost any occasion, joyful, or, as in the present case, distressing. (*All sigh.*) I have preached it at harvest celebrations, christenings, confirmations, on days of humiliation and festal days. The last time I delivered it was in the Cathedral, as a charity sermon on behalf of the Society for the Prevention of Discontent among the Upper Orders. The Bishop, who was present, was much struck by some of the analogies I drew.

JACK: Ah! that reminds me, you mentioned christenings I think, Dr. Chasuble? I suppose you know how to christen all right? (DR. CHASUBLE *looks astounded.*) I mean, of course, you are continually christening, aren't you?

MISS PRISM: It is, I regret to say, one of the Rector's most constant duties in this parish. I have often spoken to the poorer classes on the subject. But they don't seem to know what thrift is.

thrift careful management, esp. of money

CHASUBLE: But is there any particular infant in whom you are interested, Mr. Worthing? Your brother was, I believe, unmarried, was he not?

JACK: Oh yes.

MISS PRISM: (*Bitterly.*) People who live entirely for pleasure usually are.

JACK: But it is not for any child, dear Doctor. I am very fond of children. No! the fact is, I would like to be christened myself, this afternoon, if you have nothing better to do.

CHASUBLE: But surely, Mr. Worthing, you have been christened already?

JACK: I don't remember anything about it.

CHASUBLE: But have you any grave doubts on the subject?

JACK: I certainly intend to have. Of course I don't know if the thing would bother you in any way, or if you think I am a little too old now.

to bother to disturb

CHASUBLE: Not at all. The sprinkling, and, indeed, the immersion of adults is a perfectly canonical practice.

to sprinkle to scatter in drops
immersion plunging sth or sb into a liquid (here: holy water)
canonical in accordance with the laws of the church
apprehension fear

JACK: Immersion!

CHASUBLE: You need have no apprehensions. Sprinkling is all that is necessary, or indeed I think advisable. Our weather is so changeable. At what hour would you wish the ceremony performed?

JACK: Oh, I might trot round about five if that would suit you.

CHASUBLE: Perfectly, perfectly! In fact I have two similar ceremonies to perform at that time. A case of twins that occurred recently in one of the outlying cottages on your own estate.

outlying distant, far away

Poor Jenkins the carter, a most hard-working man.

JACK: Oh! I don't see much fun in being christened along with other babies. It would be childish. Would half-past five do?

CHASUBLE: Admirably! Admirably! (*Takes out watch.*) And now, dear Mr. Worthing, I will not intrude any longer into a house of sorrow. I would merely beg you not to be too much bowed down by grief. What seem to us bitter trials are often blessings in disguise.

MISS PRISM: This seems to me a blessing of an extremely obvious kind.

(*Enter* CECILY *from the house.*)

CECILY: Uncle Jack! Oh, I am pleased to see you back. But what horrid clothes you have got on! Do go and change them.

MISS PRISM: Cecily!

CHASUBLE: My child! my child! (CECILY *goes towards* JACK; *he kisses her brow in a melancholy manner.*)

CECILY: What is the matter, Uncle Jack? Do look happy! You look as if you had toothache, and I have got such a surprise for you. Who do you think is in the dining-room? Your brother!

JACK: Who?

CECILY: Your brother Ernest. He arrived about half an hour ago.

JACK: What nonsense! I haven't got a brother.

CECILY: Oh, don't say that. However badly he may have behaved to you in the past he is still your brother. You couldn't be so heartless as to disown him. I'll tell him to come out. And you will shake hands with him, won't you, Uncle Jack? (*Runs back into the house.*)

CHASUBLE: These are very joyful tidings.

MISS PRISM: After we had all been resigned to his loss, his sudden return seems to me peculiarly distressing.

JACK: My brother is in the dining-room? I don't know what it all means. I think it is perfectly absurd.

(*Enter* ALGERNON *and* CECILY *hand in hand. They come slowly up to* JACK.)

JACK: Good heavens! (*Motions* ALGERNON *away.*)

ALGERNON: Brother John, I have come down from town to tell you that I am very sorry for all the trouble I have given you, and that I intend to lead a better life in the future. (JACK *glares at him and does not take his hand.*)

CECILY: Uncle Jack, you are not going to refuse your own brother's hand?

JACK: Nothing will induce me to take his hand. I think his coming down here disgraceful. He knows perfectly well why.

carter driver of a cart

bowed down defeated; hanging one's head due to sadness or worry

disown to refuse to acknowledge a member of the family

joyful tidings news causing great happiness

to be resigned to sth to accept a difficult situation patiently

peculiar strange

disgraceful shameful, without honour

CECILY: Uncle Jack, do be nice. There is some good in every one. Ernest has just been telling me about his poor invalid friend Mr. Bunbury whom he goes to visit so often. And surely there must be much good in one who is kind to an invalid, and leaves the pleasures of London to sit by a bed of pain.

JACK: Oh! he has been talking about Bunbury, has he?

CECILY: Yes, he has told me all about poor Mr. Bunbury, and his terrible state of health.

JACK: Bunbury! Well, I won't have him talk to you about Bunbury or about anything else. It is enough to drive one perfectly frantic.

to drive sb frantic to drive sb mad

ALGERNON: Of course I admit that the faults were all on my side. But I must say that I think that Brother John's coldness to me is peculiarly painful. I expected a more enthusiastic welcome, especially considering it is the first time I have come here.

CECILY: Uncle Jack, if you don't shake hands with Ernest I will never forgive you.

JACK: Never forgive me?

CECILY: Never, never, never!

JACK: Well, this is the last time I shall ever do it. (*Shakes with* ALGERNON *and glares.*)

CHASUBLE: It's pleasant, is it not, to see so perfect a reconciliation? I think we might leave the two brothers together.

reconciliation becoming friends again after a dispute

MISS PRISM: Cecily, you will come with us.

CECILY: Certainly, Miss Prism. My little task of reconciliation is over.

CHASUBLE: You have done a beautiful action to-day, dear child.

MISS PRISM: We must not be premature in our judgments.

premature too quick

CECILY: I feel very happy. (*They all go off except* JACK *and* ALGERNON.)

JACK: You young scoundrel, Algy, you must get out of this place as soon as possible. I don't allow any Bunburying here.

scoundrel a mean or wicked person

(*Enter* MERRIMAN.)

MERRIMAN: I have put Mr. Ernest's things in the room next to yours, sir. I suppose that is all right?

JACK: What?

MERRIMAN: Mr. Ernest's luggage, sir. I have unpacked it and put it in the room next to your own.

JACK: His luggage?

MERRIMAN: Yes, sir. Three portmanteaus, a dressing-case, two hat-boxes, and a large luncheon-basket.

ALGERNON: I am afraid I can't stay more than a week this time.

JACK: Merriman, order the dog-cart at once. Mr. Ernest has been suddenly called back to town.

portmanteau a suitcase
dressing-case a bag used for carrying toiletries, i.e. toothpaste, soap, aftershave, etc.
luncheon-basket a box for one's food
dog-cart an open horse-drawn carriage

Merriman: Yes, sir. (*Goes back into the house.*)

Algernon: What a fearful liar you are, Jack. I have not been called back to town at all.

Jack: Yes, you have.

Algernon: I haven't heard any one call me.

Jack: Your duty as a gentleman calls you back.

Algernon: My duty as a gentleman has never interfered with my pleasures in the smallest degree.

Jack: I can quite understand that.

Algernon: Well, Cecily is a darling.

Jack: You are not to talk of Miss Cardew like that. I don't like it.

Algernon: Well, I don't like your clothes. You look perfectly ridiculous in them. Why on earth don't you go up and change? It is perfectly childish to be in deep mourning for a man who is actually staying for a whole week with you in your house as a guest. I call it grotesque.

Jack: You are certainly not staying with me for a whole week as a guest or anything else. You have got to leave ... by the four-five train.

Algernon: I certainly won't leave you so long as you are in mourning. It would be most unfriendly. If I were in mourning you would stay with me, I suppose. I should think it very unkind if you didn't.

Jack: Well, will you go if I change my clothes?

Algernon: Yes, if you are not too long. I never saw anybody take so long to dress, and with such little result.

Jack: Well, at any rate, that is better than being always over-dressed as you are.

Algernon: If I am occasionally a little over-dressed, I make up for it by being always immensely over-educated.

Jack: Your vanity is ridiculous, your conduct an outrage, and your presence in my garden utterly absurd. However, you have got to catch the four-five, and I hope you will have a pleasant journey back to town. This Bunburying, as you call it, has not been a great success for you.

(*Goes into the house.*)

Algernon: I think it has been a great success. I'm in love with Cecily, and that is everything.

(*Enter* Cecily *at the back of the garden. She picks up the can and begins to water the flowers.*) But I must see her before I go, and make arrangements for another Bunbury. Ah, there she is.

Cecily: Oh, I merely came back to water the roses. I thought you were with Uncle Jack.

Algernon: He's gone to order the dog-cart for me.

ridiculous laughable

grotesque very strange and unexpected

vanity a very high opinion of oneself

outrage scandal

CECILY: Oh, is he going to take you for a nice drive?

ALGERNON: He's going to send me away.

CECILY: Then have we got to part?

ALGERNON: I am afraid so. It's a very painful parting.

CECILY: It is always painful to part from people whom one has known for a very brief space of time. The absence of old friends one can endure with equanimity. But even a momentary separation from anyone to whom one has just been introduced is almost unbearable.

equanimity keeping calm in difficult situations

ALGERNON: Thank you.

(*Enter* MERRIMAN.)

MERRIMAN: The dog-cart is at the door, sir. (ALGERNON *looks appealingly at* CECILY.)

CECILY: It can wait, Merriman for … five minutes.

MERRIMAN: Yes, Miss. (*Exit* MERRIMAN.)

exit used in plays to indicate that a character leaves the stage

ALGERNON: I hope, Cecily, I shall not offend you if I state quite frankly and openly that you seem to me to be in every way the visible personification of absolute perfection.

CECILY: I think your frankness does you great credit, Ernest. If you will allow me, I will copy your remarks into my diary. (*Goes over to table and begins writing in diary.*)

personification *Personifizierung*
frankness openness
to do sb credit to give a favourable impression

ALGERNON: Do you really keep a diary? I'd give anything to look at it. May I?

CECILY: Oh no. (*Puts her hand over it.*) You see, it is simply a very young girl's record of her own thoughts and impressions, and consequently meant for publication. When it appears in volume form I hope you will order a copy. But pray, Ernest, don't stop. I delight in taking down from dictation. I have reached 'absolute perfection'. You can go on. I am quite ready for more.

Invent another entry in Cecily's diary and try to imitate Wilde's use of paradoxes.

ALGERNON: (*Somewhat taken aback.*) Ahem! Ahem!

CECILY: Oh, don't cough, Ernest. When one is dictating one should speak fluently and not cough. Besides, I don't know how to spell a cough. (*Writes as* ALGERNON *speaks.*)

to cough *husten*

ALGERNON: (*Speaking very rapidly.*) Cecily, ever since I first looked upon your wonderful and incomparable beauty, I have dared to love you wildly, passionately, devotedly, hopelessly.

CECILY: I don't think that you should tell me that you love me wildly, passionately, devotedly, hopelessly. Hopelessly doesn't seem to make much sense, does it?

ALGERNON: Cecily!

(*Enter* MERRIMAN.)

MERRIMAN: The dog-cart is waiting, sir.

ALGERNON: Tell it to come round next week, at the same hour.

MERRIMAN: (*Looks at* CECILY, *who makes no sign.*) Yes, sir.

(MERRIMAN *retires.*)

CECILY: Uncle Jack would be very much annoyed if he knew you were staying on till next week, at the same hour.

ALGERNON: Oh, I don't care about Jack. I don't care for anybody in the whole world but you. I love you, Cecily. You will marry me, won't you?

CECILY: You silly boy! Of course. Why, we have been engaged for the last three months.

ALGERNON: For the last three months?

CECILY: Yes, it will be exactly three months on Thursday.

ALGERNON: But how did we become engaged?

CECILY: Well, ever since dear Uncle Jack first confessed to us that he had a younger brother who was very wicked and bad, you of course have formed the chief topic of conversation between myself and Miss Prism. And of course a man who is much talked about is always very attractive. One feels there must be something in him, after all. I daresay it was foolish of me, but I fell in love with you, Ernest.

chief main

I daresay I suppose

ALGERNON: Darling! And when was the engagement actually settled?

CECILY: On the 14th of February last. Worn out by your entire ignorance of my existence, I determined to end the matter one way or the other, and after a long struggle with myself I accepted you under this dear old tree here. The next day I bought this little ring in your name, and this is the little bangle with the true lover's knot I promised you always to wear.

worn out tired, lacking energy

bangle a band worn around the wrist

ALGERNON: Did I give you this? It's very pretty, isn't it?

CECILY: Yes, you've wonderfully good taste, Ernest. It's the excuse I've always given for your leading such a bad life. And this is the box in which I keep all your dear letters. (*Kneels at table, opens box, and produces letters tied up with blue ribbon.*)

ribbon a narrow strip of material e.g. silk for tying sth

ALGERNON: My letters! But, my own sweet Cecily, I have never written you any letters.

CECILY: You need hardly remind me of that, Ernest. I remember only too well that I was forced to write your letters for you. I wrote always three times a week, and sometimes oftener.

ALGERNON: Oh, do let me read them, Cecily?

CECILY: Oh, I couldn't possibly. They would make you far too conceited. (*Replaces box.*) The three you wrote me after I had broken off the engagement are so beautiful, and so badly spelled, that even now I can hardly read them without crying a little.

conceited proud of one's abilities or looks

ALGERNON: But was our engagement ever broken off?

CECILY: Of course it was. On the 22nd of last March. You can see the entry if you like. (*Shows diary.*) 'To-day I broke off my engagement with Ernest. I feel it is better to do so. The weather still continues charming.'

ALGERNON: But why on earth did you break it off? What had I done? I had done nothing at all. Cecily, I am very much hurt indeed to hear you broke it off. Particularly when the weather was so charming.

CECILY: It would hardly have been a really serious engagement if it hadn't been broken off at least once. But I forgave you before the week was out.

ALGERNON: (*Crossing to her, and kneeling.*) What a perfect angel you are, Cecily.

CECILY: You dear romantic boy. (*He kisses her, she puts her fingers through his hair.*) I hope your hair curls naturally, does it?

ALGERNON: Yes, darling, with a little help from others.

CECILY: I am so glad.

ALGERNON: You'll never break off our engagement again, Cecily?

CECILY: I don't think I could break it off now that I have actually met you. Besides, of course, there is the question of your name.

ALGERNON: Yes, of course. (*Nervously.*)

CECILY: You must not laugh at me, darling, but it had always been a girlish dream of mine to love some one whose name was Ernest. (ALGERNON *rises,* CECILY *also.*) There is something in that name that seems to inspire absolute confidence. I pity any poor married woman whose husband is not called Ernest.

ALGERNON: But, my dear child, do you mean to say you could not love me if I had some other name?

CECILY: But what name?

ALGERNON: Oh, any name you like – Algernon – for instance ...

CECILY: But I don't like the name of Algernon.

ALGERNON: Well, my own dear, sweet, loving little darling, I really can't see why you should object to the name of Algernon. It is not at all a bad name. In fact, it is rather an aristocratic name. Half of the chaps who get into the Bankruptcy Court are called Algernon. But seriously, Cecily ... (*Moving to her.*) ... if my name was Algy, couldn't you love me?

chap (coll.) man
Bankruptcy Court *Konkursgericht*

CECILY: (*Rising.*) I might respect you, Ernest, I might admire your character, but I fear that I should not be able to give you my undivided attention.

ALGERNON: Ahem! Cecily! (*Picking up hat.*) Your Rector here is, I suppose, thoroughly experienced in the practice of all the rites and ceremonials of the Church?

CECILY: Oh, yes. Dr. Chasuble is a most learned man. He has never written a single book, so you can imagine how much he knows.

ALGERNON: I must see him at once on a most important christening – I mean on most important business.

CECILY: Oh!

ALGERNON: I shan't be away more than half an hour.

CECILY: Considering that we have been engaged since February the 14th, and that I only met you to-day for the first time, I think it is rather hard that you should leave me for so long a period as half an hour. Couldn't you make it twenty minutes?

ALGERNON: I'll be back in no time.

(*Kisses her and rushes down the garden.*)

CECILY: What an impetuous boy he is! I like his hair so much. I must enter his proposal in my diary.

(*Enter* MERRIMAN.)

MERRIMAN: A Miss Fairfax has just called to see Mr. Worthing. On very important business, Miss Fairfax states.

CECILY: Isn't Mr. Worthing in his library?

MERRIMAN: Mr. Worthing went over in the direction of the Rectory some time ago.

CECILY: Pray ask the lady to come out here; Mr. Worthing is sure to be back soon. And you can bring tea.

MERRIMAN: Yes, Miss. (*Goes out.*)

CECILY: Miss Fairfax! I suppose one of the many good elderly women who are associated with Uncle Jack in some of his philanthropic work in London. I don't quite like women who are interested in philanthropic work. I think it is so forward of them.

(*Enter* MERRIMAN.)

MERRIMAN: Miss Fairfax.

(*Enter* GWENDOLEN.)

(*Exit* MERRIMAN.)

CECILY: (*Advancing to meet her.*) Pray let me introduce myself to you. My name is Cecily Cardew.

GWENDOLEN: Cecily Cardew? (*Moving to her and shaking hands.*) What a very sweet name! Something tells me that we are going to be great friends. I like you already more than I can say. My first impressions of people are never wrong.

CECILY: How nice of you to like me so much after we have known each other such a comparatively short time. Pray sit down.

ceremonial a special ceremony for a particular event, such as a christening

impetuous taking quick action without careful thought, impulsive, rash

Rectory the house where a rector, i.e. a priest lives

elderly somewhat old, past middle age

philanthropic charitable, giving generously to help other people
philanthropist
philanthropy

GWENDOLEN: (*Still standing up.*) I may call you Cecily, may I not?

CECILY: With pleasure!

GWENDOLEN: And you will always call me Gwendolen, won't you?

CECILY: If you wish.

GWENDOLEN: Then that is all quite settled, is it not?

CECILY: I hope so. (*A pause. They both sit down together.*)

GWENDOLEN: Perhaps this might be a favourable opportunity for my mentioning who I am. My father is Lord Bracknell. You have never heard of papa, I suppose?

CECILY: I don't think so.

Find out something about the Victorian concept of the "angel in the house" and compare this to Gwendolen's opinions.

sphere a field of influence or activity

effeminate having qualities that are regarded as typical for women

GWENDOLEN: Outside the family circle, papa, I am glad to say, is entirely unknown. I think that is quite as it should be. The home seems to me to be the proper sphere for the man. And certainly once a man begins to neglect his domestic duties he becomes painfully effeminate, does he not? And I don't like that. It makes men so very attractive. Cecily, mamma, whose views on education are remarkably strict, has brought me up to be extremely short-sighted; it is part of her system; so do you mind my looking at you through my glasses?

CECILY: Oh! not at all, Gwendolen. I am very fond of being looked at.

lorgnette *Lorgnette, Handbrille*

GWENDOLEN: (*After examining* CECILY *carefully through a lorgnette.*) You are here on a short visit, I suppose.

CECILY: Oh no! I live here.

to reside to live in a particular place, usually for a long period

GWENDOLEN: (*Severely.*) Really? Your mother, no doubt, or some female relative of advanced years, resides here also?

CECILY: Oh no! I have no mother, nor, in fact, any relations.

GWENDOLEN: Indeed?

arduous difficult

CECILY: My dear guardian, with the assistance of Miss Prism, has the arduous task of looking after me.

GWENDOLEN: Your guardian?

CECILY: Yes, I am Mr. Worthing's ward.

alluring attractive in an exciting and mysterious way

GWENDOLEN: Oh! It is strange he never mentioned to me that he had a ward. How secretive of him! He grows more interesting hourly. I am not sure, however, that the news inspires me with feelings of unmixed delight. (*Rising and going to her.*) I am very fond of you, Cecily; I have liked you ever since I met you! But I am bound to state that now that I know that you are Mr. Worthing's ward, I cannot help expressing a wish you were – well, just a little older than you seem to be – and not quite so very alluring in appearance. In fact, if I may speak candidly –

CECILY: Pray do! I think that whenever one has anything unpleasant to say, one should always be quite candid.

GWENDOLEN: Well, to speak with perfect candour, Cecily, I wish that you were fully forty-two, and more than usually plain for your age. Ernest has a strong upright nature. He is the very soul of truth and honour. Disloyalty would be as impossible to him as deception. But even men of the noblest possible moral character are extremely susceptible to the influence of the physical charms of others. Modern, no less than Ancient History, supplies us with many most painful examples of what I refer to. If it were not so, indeed, History would be quite unreadable.

CECILY: I beg your pardon, Gwendolen, did you say Ernest?

GWENDOLEN: Yes.

CECILY: Oh, but it is not Mr. Ernest Worthing who is my guardian. It is his brother – his elder brother.

GWENDOLEN: (*Sitting down again.*) Ernest never mentioned to me that he had a brother.

CECILY: I am sorry to say they have not been on good terms for a long time.

GWENDOLEN: Ah! that accounts for it. And now that I think of it I have never heard any man mention his brother. The subject seems distasteful to most men. Cecily, you have lifted a load from my mind. I was growing almost anxious. It would have been terrible if any cloud had come across a friendship like ours, would it not? Of course you are quite, quite sure that it is not Mr. Ernest Worthing who is your guardian?

CECILY: Quite sure. (*A pause.*) In fact, I am going to be his.

GWENDOLEN: (*Enquiringly.*) I beg your pardon?

CECILY: (*Rather shy and confidingly.*) Dearest Gwendolen, there is no reason why I should make a secret of it to you. Our little county newspaper is sure to chronicle the fact next week. Mr. Ernest Worthing and I are engaged to be married.

GWENDOLEN: (*Quite politely, rising.*) My darling Cecily, I think there must be some slight error. Mr. Ernest Worthing is engaged to me. The announcement will appear in the *Morning Post* on Saturday at the latest.

CECILY: (*Very politely, rising.*) I am afraid you must be under some misconception. Ernest proposed to me exactly ten minutes ago. (*Shows diary.*)

GWENDOLEN: (*Examines diary through her lorgnette carefully.*) It is certainly very curious, for he asked me to be his wife yesterday afternoon at 5.30. If you would care to verify the incident, pray do so. (*Produces diary of her own.*) I never travel without my diary. One should always have something sensational to read in the train. I am so sorry, dear Cecily, if it is any disappointment to you, but I am afraid I have the prior claim.

candid open
candour

disloyalty unfaithfulness

charm the power to attract or please

enquiring curious, trying to find out
confiding showing trust and confidence by telling secrets

misconception wrong impression or belief

to verify to prove that sth is true

prior earlier

Cecily: It would distress me more than I can tell you, dear Gwendolen, if it caused you any mental or physical anguish, but I feel bound to point out that since Ernest proposed to you he clearly has changed his mind.

Gwendolen: (*Meditatively.*) If the poor fellow has been entrapped into any foolish promise I shall consider it my duty to rescue him at once, and with a firm hand.

Cecily: (*Thoughtfully and sadly.*) Whatever unfortunate entanglement my dear boy may have got into, I will never reproach him with it after we are married.

Gwendolen: Do you allude to me, Miss Cardew, as an entanglement? You are presumptuous. On an occasion of this kind it becomes more than a moral duty to speak one's mind. It becomes a pleasure.

Cecily: Do you suggest, Miss Fairfax, that I entrapped Ernest into an engagement? How dare you? This is no time for wearing the shallow mask of manners. When I see a spade I call it a spade.

Gwendolen: (*Satirically.*) I am glad to say that I have never seen a spade. It is obvious that our social spheres have been widely different.

(*Enter* Merriman, *followed by the footman. He carries a salver, table cloth, and plate stand.* Cecily *is about to retort. The presence of the servants exercises a restraining influence, under which both girls chafe.*)

Merriman: Shall I lay tea here as usual, Miss?

Cecily: (*Sternly, in a calm voice.*) Yes, as usual. (Merriman *begins to clear table and lay cloth. A long pause.* Cecily *and* Gwendolen *glare at each other.*)

Gwendolen: Are there many interesting walks in the vicinity, Miss Cardew?

Cecily: Oh! yes! a great many. From the top of one of the hills quite close one can see five counties.

Gwendolen: Five counties! I don't think I should like that; I hate crowds.

Cecily: (*Sweetly.*) I suppose that is why you live in town? (Gwendolen *bites her lip, and beats her foot nervously with her parasol.*)

Gwendolen: (*Looking round.*) Quite a well-kept garden this is, Miss Cardew.

Cecily: So glad you like it, Miss Fairfax.

Gwendolen: I had no idea there were any flowers in the country.

Cecily: Oh, flowers are as common here, Miss Fairfax, as people are in London.

Gwendolen: Personally I cannot understand how anybody

anguish suffering
meditative deeply thoughtful
entrapped caught in a trap
entanglement act of becoming mixed or twisted up in sth or with sb else
to reproach to blame or criticize
to allude to to refer to sth indirectly
presumptuous going beyond what is proper
to call a spade a spade (idiom) to say exactly what you really think
footman a manservant similar to a butler
to retort to reply angrily or sharply
to chafe to be bothered and impatient
stern hard and severe
vicinity neighbourhood
parasol an umbrella that protects against sunlight
common widespread; in this context, the term refers to something of inferior quality, and with reference to people it means that they are low-class, vulgar, or ordinary

manages to exist in the country, if anybody who is anybody does. The country always bores me to death.

CECILY: Ah! This is what the newspapers call agricultural depression, is it not? I believe the aristocracy are suffering very much from it just at present. It is almost an epidemic amongst them, I have been told. May I offer you some tea, Miss Fairfax?

GWENDOLEN: (*With elaborate politeness.*) Thank you. (*Aside.*) Detestable girl! But I require tea!

CECILY: (*Sweetly.*) Sugar?

GWENDOLEN: (*Superciliously.*) No, thank you. Sugar is not fashionable any more. (CECILY *looks angrily at her, takes up the tongs and puts four lumps of sugar into the cup.*)

CECILY: (*Severely.*) Cake or bread and butter?

GWENDOLEN: (*In a bored manner.*) Bread and butter, please. Cake is rarely seen at the best houses nowadays.

CECILY: (*Cuts a very large slice of cake, and puts it on the tray.*) Hand that to Miss Fairfax.

(MERRIMAN *does so, and goes out with footman.* GWENDOLEN *drinks the tea and makes a grimace. Puts down cup at once, reaches out her hand to the bread and butter, looks at it, and finds it is cake. Rises in indignation.)*

GWENDOLEN: You have filled my tea with lumps of sugar, and though I asked most distinctly for bread and butter, you have given me cake. I am known for the gentleness of my disposition, and the extraordinary sweetness of my nature, but I warn you, Miss Cardew, you may go too far.

CECILY: (*Rising.*) To save my poor, innocent, trusting boy from the machinations of any other girl there are no lengths to which I would not go.

GWENDOLEN: From the moment I saw you I distrusted you. I felt that you were false and deceitful. I am never deceived in such matters. My first impressions of people are invariably right.

CECILY: It seems to me, Miss Fairfax, that I am trespassing on your valuable time. No doubt you have many other calls of a similar character to make in the neighbourhood.

(*Enter* JACK.)

GWENDOLEN: (*Catching sight of him.*) Ernest! My own Ernest!

JACK: Gwendolen! Darling! (*Offers to kiss her.*)

GWENDOLEN: (*Draws back.*) A moment! May I ask if you are engaged to be married to this young lady? (*Points to* CECILY.)

JACK: (*Laughing.*) To dear little Cecily! Of course not! What could have put such an idea into your pretty little head?

GWENDOLEN: Thank you. You may! (*Offers her cheek.*)

CECILY: (*Very sweetly.*) I knew there must be some misunderstanding, Miss Fairfax. The gentleman whose arm is at pre-

agricultural depression
The newspapers are referring to economic depression but the young ladies interpret it as emotional depression.

elaborate here: overdone, exaggerated
detestable causing or deserving strong dislike or hatred
supercilious thinking that others are of little importance
tongs *Zange*

machinations clever plans for harming sb
to go to some lengths to make great efforts

deceitful dishonest, untrustworthy
deceitfulness
to deceive
deceiver
deception

to trespass on sth to make unfair or unreasonable use of

sent round your waist is my guardian, Mr. John Worthing.

GWENDOLEN: I beg your pardon?

CECILY: This is Uncle Jack.

GWENDOLEN: (*Receding.*) Jack! Oh!

(*Enter* ALGERNON.)

CECILY: Here is Ernest.

ALGERNON: (*Goes straight over to* CECILY *without noticing any one else.*) My own love! (*Offers to kiss her.*)

CECILY: (*Drawing back.*) A moment, Ernest! May I ask you – are you engaged to be married to this young lady?

ALGERNON: (*Looking round.*) To what young lady? Good heavens! Gwendolen!

CECILY: Yes! to good heavens, Gwendolen, I mean to Gwendolen.

ALGERNON: (*Laughing.*) Of course not! What could have put such an idea into your pretty little head?

CECILY: Thank you. (*Presenting her cheek to be kissed.*) You may. (ALGERNON *kisses her.*)

GWENDOLEN: I felt there was some slight error, Miss Cardew. The gentleman who is now embracing you is my cousin, Mr. Algernon Moncrieff.

to embrace to encircle with the arms, to hug

CECILY: (*Breaking away from* ALGERNON.) Algernon Moncrieff! Oh! (*The two girls move towards each other and put their arms round each other's waists as if for protection.*)

CECILY: Are you called Algernon?

ALGERNON: I cannot deny it.

CECILY: Oh!

GWENDOLEN: Is your name really John?

JACK: (*Standing rather proudly.*) I could deny it if I liked. I could deny anything if I liked. But my name certainly is John. It has been John for years.

to deny to say sth is not true

CECILY: (*To* GWENDOLEN.) A gross deception has been practised on both of us.

GWENDOLEN: My poor wounded Cecily!

CECILY: My sweet wronged Gwendolen!

GWENDOLEN: (*Slowly and seriously.*) You will call me sister, will you not? (*They embrace.* JACK *and* ALGERNON *groan and walk up and down.*)

CECILY: (*Rather brightly.*) There is just one question I would like to be allowed to ask my guardian.

GWENDOLEN: An admirable idea! Mr. Worthing, there is just one question I would like to be permitted to put to you. Where is your brother Ernest? We are both engaged to be married to your brother Ernest, so it is a matter of some importance to us to know where your brother Ernest is at present.

JACK: (*Slowly and hesitatingly.*) Gwendolen – Cecily – it is very painful for me to be forced to speak the truth. It is the first time in my life that I have ever been reduced to such a painful position, and I am really quite inexperienced in doing anything of the kind. However, I will tell you quite frankly that I have no brother Ernest. I have no brother at all. I never had a brother in my life, and I certainly have not the smallest intention of ever having one in the future.

CECILY: (*Surprised.*) No brother at all?

JACK: (*Cheerily.*) None!

GWENDOLEN: (*Severely.*) Had you never a brother of any kind?

JACK: (*Pleasantly.*) Never. Not even of an kind.

GWENDOLEN: I am afraid it is quite clear, Cecily, that neither of us is engaged to be married to any one.

CECILY: It is not a very pleasant position for a young girl suddenly to find herself in. Is it?

GWENDOLEN: Let us go into the house. They will hardly venture to come after us there.

CECILY: No, men are so cowardly, aren't they?

(*They retire into the house with scornful looks.*)

JACK: This ghastly state of things is what you call Bunburying, I suppose?

ALGERNON: Yes, and a perfectly wonderful Bunbury it is. The most wonderful Bunbury I have ever had in my life.

JACK: Well, you've no right whatsoever to Bunbury here.

ALGERNON: That is absurd. One has a right to Bunbury anywhere one chooses. Every serious Bunburyist knows that.

JACK: Serious Bunburyist! Good heavens!

ALGERNON: Well, one must be serious about something, if one wants to have any amusement in life. I happen to be serious about Bunburying. What on earth you are serious about I haven't got the remotest idea. About everything, I should fancy. You have such an absolutely trivial nature.

JACK: Well, the only small satisfaction I have in the whole of this wretched business is that your friend Bunbury is quite exploded. You won't be able to run down to the country quite so often as you used to do, dear Algy. And a very good thing too.

ALGERNON: Your brother is a little off colour, isn't he, dear Jack? You won't be able to disappear to London quite so frequently as your wicked custom was. And not a bad thing either.

JACK: As for your conduct towards Miss Cardew, I must say that your taking in a sweet, simple, innocent girl like that is quite inexcusable. To say nothing of the fact that she is my ward.

ALGERNON: I can see no possible defence at all for your deceiv-

to venture to do sth even though it is dangerous or unpleasant

cowardly behaving like a coward, i.e. a person who shows dishonourable fear
coward
cowardice ['kaʊədɪs]

scornful showing or feeling scorn, i.e. a mixture of disgust and anger

to fancy to imagine

wretched very unhappy, unfortunate

off colour not well, sick

custom here: habit

conduct behaviour

to take sb in to deceive, to fool

ing a brilliant, clever, thoroughly experienced young lady like Miss Fairfax. To say nothing of the fact that she is my cousin.

JACK: I wanted to be engaged to Gwendolen, that is all. I love her.

ALGERNON: Well, I simply wanted to be engaged to Cecily. I adore her.

JACK: There is certainly no chance of your marrying Miss Cardew.

ALGERNON: I don't think there is much likelihood, Jack, of you and Miss Fairfax being united.

JACK: Well, that is no business of yours.

ALGERNON: If it was my business, I wouldn't talk about it. (*Begins to eat muffins.*) It is very vulgar to talk about one's business. Only people like stockbrokers do that, and then merely at dinner parties.

stockbroker a person who handles orders to sell and buy stocks on the stock market

JACK: How can you sit there, calmly eating muffins when we are in this horrible trouble, I can't make out. You seem to me to be perfectly heartless.

ALGERNON: Well, I can't eat muffins in an agitated manner. The butter would probably get on my cuffs. One should always eat muffins quite calmly. It is the only way to eat them.

JACK: I say it's perfectly heartless your eating muffins at all, under the circumstances.

ALGERNON: When I am in trouble, eating is the only thing that consoles me. Indeed, when I am in really great trouble, as any one who knows me intimately will tell you, I refuse everything except food and drink. At the present moment I am eating muffins because I am unhappy. Besides, I am particularly fond of muffins. (*Rising.*)

to console sb to make sb feel better

JACK: (*Rising.*) Well, that is no reason why you should eat them all in that greedy way. (*Takes muffins from* ALGERNON.)

greedy wanting more of sth than you really need

ALGERNON: (*Offering tea-cake.*) I wish you would have tea-cake instead. I don't like tea-cake.

JACK: Good heavens! I suppose a man may eat his own muffins in his own garden.

ALGERNON: But you have just said it was perfectly heartless to eat muffins.

JACK: I said it was perfectly heartless of you, under the circumstances. That is a very different thing.

ALGERNON: That may be. But the muffins are the same. (*He seizes the muffin-dish from* JACK.)

to seize to take sth suddenly and using force

JACK: Algy, I wish to goodness you would go.

ALGERNON: You can't possibly ask me to go without having some dinner. It's absurd. I never go without my dinner. No one ever does, except vegetarians and people like that. Besides I have just made arrangements with Dr. Chasuble to be christened at a quarter to six under the name of Ernest.

JACK: My dear fellow, the sooner you give up that nonsense the better. I made arrangements this morning with Dr. Chasuble to be christened myself at 5.30, and I naturally will take the name of Ernest. Gwendolen would wish it. We can't both be christened Ernest. It's absurd. Besides, I have a perfect right to be christened if I like. There is no evidence at all that I have ever been christened by anybody. I should think it extremely probable I never was, and so does Dr. Chasuble. It is entirely different in your case. You have been christened already.

ALGERNON: Yes, but I have not been christened for years.

JACK: Yes, but you have been christened. That is the important thing.

ALGERNON: Quite so. So I know my constitution can stand it. If you are not quite sure about your ever having been christened, I must say I think it rather dangerous your venturing on it now. It might make you very unwell. You can hardly have forgotten that some one very closely connected with you was very nearly carried off this week in Paris by a severe chill.

constitution the condition of a person's body, health

to venture to do sth even though it is dangerous or unpleasant

JACK: Yes, but you said yourself that a severe chill was not hereditary.

ALGERNON: It usen't to be, I know – but I daresay it is now. Science is always making wonderful improvements in things.

JACK: (*Picking up the muffin-dish.*) Oh, that is nonsense; you are always talking nonsense.

ALGERNON: Jack, you are at the muffins again! I wish you wouldn't. There are only two left. (*Takes them.*) I told you I was particularly fond of muffins.

JACK: But I hate tea-cake.

ALGERNON: Why on earth then do you allow tea-cake to be served up for your guests? What ideas you have of hospitality!

hospitality friendly behaviour towards guests

JACK: Algernon! I have already told you to go. I don't want you here. Why don't you go!

ALGERNON: I haven't quite finished my tea yet! And there is still one muffin left. (JACK *groans, and sinks into a chair.* ALGERNON *still continues eating.*)

ACT-DROP

Act III

Scene – Morning-room at the Manor House.

(GWENDOLEN *and* CECILY *are at the window, looking out into the garden.*)

GWENDOLEN: The fact that they did not follow us at once into the house, as any one else would have done, seems to me to show that they have some sense of shame left.

repentance the act of showing you feel sorry for sth done
to repent
repentant

CECILY: They have been eating muffins. That looks like repentance.

GWENDOLEN: (*After a pause.*) They don't seem to notice us at all. Couldn't you cough?

Explain the function of food and eating in the play.

CECILY: But I haven't got a cough.

effrontery rudeness without any sense of shame

GWENDOLEN: They're looking at us. What effrontery!

forward too sure of oneself

CECILY: They're approaching. That's very forward of them.

dignified calm, serious, deserving respect

GWENDOLEN: Let us preserve a dignified silence.

air here: melody or song

CECILY: Certainly. It's the only thing to do now. (*Enter* JACK *followed by* ALGERNON. *They whistle some dreadful popular air from a British Opera.*)

British Opera Oscar Wilde is most probably referring to the comic opera *Patience* by Sir William S. Gilbert and Sir Arthur Sullivan in which he was satirically characterized.

GWENDOLEN: This dignified silence seems to produce an unpleasant effect.

CECILY: A most distasteful one.

GWENDOLEN: But we will not be the first to speak.

CECILY: Certainly not.

GWENDOLEN: Mr. Worthing, I have something very particular to ask you. Much depends on your reply.

invaluable worth a lot

CECILY: Gwendolen, your common sense is invaluable. Mr. Moncrieff, kindly answer me the following question. Why did you pretend to be my guardian's brother?

to pretend to be sth or sb that you are not

ALGERNON: In order that I might have an opportunity of meeting you.

CECILY: (*To* GWENDOLEN.) That certainly seems a satisfactory explanation, does it not?

GWENDOLEN: Yes, dear, if you can believe him.

CECILY: I don't. But that does not affect the wonderful beauty of his answer.

sincerity honesty

GWENDOLEN: True. In matters of grave importance, style, not sincerity is the vital thing. Mr. Worthing, what explanation can you offer to me for pretending to have a brother? Was it in order that you might have an opportunity of coming up to town to see me as often as possible?

JACK: Can you doubt it, Miss Fairfax?

GWENDOLEN: I have the gravest doubts upon the subject. But I intend to crush them. This is not the moment for German scepticism. (*Moving to* Cecily.) Their explanations appear to be quite satisfactory, especially Mr. Worthing's. That seems to me to have the stamp of truth upon it.

Cecily: I am more than content with what Mr. Moncrieff said. His voice alone inspires one with absolute credulity.

Gwendolen: Then you think we should forgive them?

Cecily: Yes. I mean no.

Gwendolen: True! I had forgotten. There are principles at stake that one cannot surrender. Which of us should tell them? The task is not a pleasant one.

Cecily: Could we not both speak at the same time?

Gwendolen: An excellent idea! I nearly always speak at the same time as other people. Will you take the time from me?

Cecily: Certainly. (Gwendolen *beats time with uplifted finger.*)

Gwendolen *and* Cecily: (*Speaking together.*) Your Christian names are still an insuperable barrier. That is all!

Jack and Algernon (*Speaking together.*) Our Christian names! Is that all? But we are going to be christened this afternoon.

Gwendolen: (*To* Jack.) For my sake you are prepared to do this terrible thing?

Jack: I am.

Cecily: (*To* Algernon.) To please me you are ready to face this fearful ordeal?

Algernon: I am!

Gwendolen: How absurd to talk of the equality of the sexes! Where questions of self-sacrifice are concerned, men are infinitely beyond us.

Jack: We are. (*Clasps hands with* Algernon.)

Cecily: They have moments of physical courage of which we women know absolutely nothing.

Gwendolen: (*To* Jack.) Darling!

Algernon: (*To* Cecily.) Darling! (*They fall into each other's arms.*)

(*Enter* Merriman. *When he enters he coughs loudly, seeing the situation.*)

Merriman: Ahem! Ahem! Lady Bracknell!

Jack: Good heavens!

(*Enter* Lady Bracknell. *The couples separate in alarm. Exit* Merriman.)

Lady Bracknell: Gwendolen! What does this mean?

Gwendolen: Merely that I am engaged to be married to Mr. Worthing, mamma.

Lady Bracknell: Come here. Sit down. Sit down immediately. Hesitation of any kind is a sign of mental decay in the young,

to crush to suppress

German scepticism refers to the tendency, here ascribed to German thinkers, to criticize or doubt the truth of certain facts, such as in the Bible

credulity believing sth very quickly without any good reasons

at stake at risk, dependent on what happens

to surrender to give up

insuperable unable to be overcome

barrier sth that blocks the way

ordeal a severe test

decay gradual destruction or decline

to apprise to inform, to make known
flight here: running away
confidence here: secret
luggage train a long distance interregional train

University Extension Scheme a plan to give women the opportunity to attend evening classes at one of the universities; Wilde once humorously suggested that its mission should be "to tell people what not to read"
to undeceive to tell the truth
to cease to stop

of physical weakness in the old. (*Turns to* JACK.) Apprised, sir, of my daughter's sudden flight by her trusty maid, whose confidence I purchased by means of a small coin, I followed her at once by a luggage train. Her unhappy father is, I am glad to say, under the impression that she is attending a more than usually lengthy lecture by the University Extension Scheme on the Influence of a permanent income on Thought. I do not propose to undeceive him. Indeed I have never undeceived him on any question. I would consider it wrong. But of course, you will clearly understand that all communication between yourself and my daughter must cease immediately from this moment. On this point, as indeed on all points, I am firm.

JACK: I am engaged to be married to Gwendolen, Lady Bracknell!

LADY BRACKNELL: You are nothing of the kind, sir. And now, as regards Algernon! ... Algernon!

ALGERNON: Yes, Aunt Augusta.

LADY BRACKNELL: May I ask if it is in this house that your invalid friend Mr. Bunbury resides?

ALGERNON: (*Stammering.*) Oh! No! Bunbury doesn't live here. Bunbury is somewhere else at present. In fact, Bunbury is dead.

LADY BRACKNELL: Dead! When did Mr. Bunbury die? His death must have been extremely sudden.

airily carefree, casual

ALGERNON: (*Airily.*) Oh! I killed Bunbury this afternoon. I mean poor Bunbury died this afternoon.

LADY BRACKNELL: What did he die of?

ALGERNON: Bunbury? Oh, he was quite exploded.

To what extent can Oscar Wilde's epigrammatic style be interpreted as a form of social criticism?

outrage here: an act of violence
morbidity unhealthy interest in unpleasant things
to be found out to be discovered, usually in a dishonest act

LADY BRACKNELL: Exploded! Was he the victim of a revolutionary outrage? I was not aware that Mr. Bunbury was interested in social legislation. If so, he is well punished for his morbidity.

ALGERNON: My dear Aunt Augusta, I mean he was found out! The doctors found out that Bunbury could not live, that is what I mean – so Bunbury died.

LADY BRACKNELL: He seems to have had great confidence in the opinion of his physicians. I am glad, however, that he made up his mind at the last to some definite course of action, and acted under proper medical advice. And now that we have finally got rid of this Mr. Bunbury, may I ask, Mr. Worthing, who is that young person whose hand my nephew Algernon is now holding in what seems to me a peculiarly unnecessary manner?

JACK: That lady is Miss Cecily Cardew, my ward. (LADY BRACKNELL *bows coldly to* CECILY.)

ALGERNON: I am engaged to be married to Cecily, Aunt Augusta.

LADY BRACKNELL: I beg your pardon?

CECILY: Mr. Moncrieff and I are engaged to be married, Lady Bracknell.

LADY BRACKNELL: (*With a shiver, crossing to the sofa and sitting down.*) I do not know whether there is anything peculiarly exciting in the air of this particular part of Hertfordshire, but the number of engagements that go on seems to me considerably above the proper average that statistics have laid down for our guidance. I think some preliminary inquiry on my part would not be out of place. Mr. Worthing, is Miss Cardew at all connected with any of the larger railway stations in London? I merely desire information. Until yesterday I had no idea that there were any families or persons whose origin was a Terminus. (JACK *looks perfectly furious, but restrains himself.*)

JACK: (*In a clear, cold voice.*) Miss Cardew is the grand-daughter of the late Mr. Thomas Cardew of 149 Belgrave Square, S.W.; Gervase Park, Dorking, Surrey; and the Sporran, Fifeshire, N.B.

LADY BRACKNELL: That sounds not unsatisfactory. Three addresses always inspire confidence, even in tradesmen. But what proof have I of their authenticity?

JACK: I have carefully preserved the Court Guides of the period. They are open to your inspection, Lady Bracknell.

LADY BRACKNELL: (*Grimly.*) I have known strange errors in that publication.

JACK: Miss Cardew's family solicitors are Messrs. Markby, Markby, and Markby.

LADY BRACKNELL: Markby, Markby, and Markby? A firm of the very highest position in their profession. Indeed I am told that one of the Mr. Markby's is occasionally to be seen at dinner parties. So far I am satisfied.

JACK: (*Very irritably.*) How extremely kind of you, Lady Bracknell! I have also in my possession, you will be pleased to hear, certificates of Miss Cardew's birth, baptism, whooping cough, registration, vaccination, confirmation, and the measles; both the German and the English variety.

LADY BRACKNELL: Ah! A life crowded with incident, I see; though perhaps somewhat too exciting for a young girl. I am not myself in favour of premature experiences. (*Rises, looks at her watch.*) Gwendolen! the time approaches for our departure. We have not a moment to lose. As a matter of form, Mr. Worthing, I had better ask you if Miss Cardew has any little fortune?

preliminary initial, coming before the main part

terminus station at the end of a railway line

late now dead

Sporran is not a real place but instead refers to the bag worn in front of a Scottish kilt, an allusion to the fact that Jack Worthing was found in a bag.

Fifeshire is a county of east central Scotland.
authenticity the fact that sth is true
to preserve to keep
Court Guide a book (directory) containing the names of all the nobles members of high society who have appeared at court
grim harsh
solicitor lawyer

irritable annoyed, bad tempered

baptism christening; *Taufe*
whooping cough *Keuchhusten*
vaccination *Impfung*
measles *Masern*

premature before the right time

as a matter of form in keeping with the usual way of doing things

Funds investments supported by the Bank of England

Explain what kind of values are most important to Lady Bracknell.

to improve to get better

surface the outside of an object

to alter to change

marvellous wonderful

to recommend to tell sb that sth or sb is good

profile view of the face seen from the side

distinct clear

twopence (also: tuppence); two pennies, thus very little

debt [det] money owed to sb else

mercenary interested mainly in money, doing sth only for money

JACK: Oh! about a hundred and thirty thousand pounds in the Funds. That is all. Goodbye, Lady Bracknell. So pleased to have seen you.

LADY BRACKNELL: (*Sitting down again.*) A moment, Mr. Worthing. A hundred and thirty thousand pounds! And in the Funds! Miss Cardew seems to me a most attractive young lady, now that I look at her. Few girls of the present day have any really solid qualities, any of the qualities that last, and improve with time. We live, I regret to say, in an age of surfaces. (*To* CECILY.) Come over here, dear. (CECILY *goes across.*) Pretty child! your dress is sadly simple, and your hair seems almost as Nature might have left it. But we can soon alter all that. A thoroughly experienced French maid produces a really marvellous result in a very brief space of time. I remember recommending one to young Lady Lancing, and after three months her own husband did not know her.

JACK: And after six months nobody knew her.

LADY BRACKNELL: (*Glares at* JACK *for a few moments. Then bends, with a practised smile, to* CECILY.) Kindly turn round, sweet child. (CECILY *turns completely round.*) No, the side view is what I want. (CECILY *presents her profile.*) Yes, quite as I expected. There are distinct social possibilities in your profile. The two weak points in our age are its want of principle and its want of profile. The chin a little higher, dear. Style largely depends on the way the chin is worn. They are worn very high, just at present. Algernon!

ALGERNON: Yes, Aunt Augusta!

LADY BRACKNELL: There are distinct social possibilities in Miss Cardew's profile.

ALGERNON: Cecily is the sweetest, dearest, prettiest girl in the whole world. And I don't care twopence about social possibilities.

LADY BRACKNELL: Never speak disrespectfully of Society, Algernon. Only people who can't get into it do that. (*To* CECILY.) Dear child, of course you know that Algernon has nothing but his debts to depend upon. But I do not approve of mercenary marriages. When I married Lord Bracknell I had no fortune of any kind. But I never dreamed for a moment of allowing that to stand in my way. Well, I suppose I must give my consent.

ALGERNON: Thank you, Aunt Augusta.

LADY BRACKNELL: Cecily, you may kiss me!

CECILY: (*Kisses her.*) Thank you, Lady Bracknell.

LADY BRACKNELL: You may also address me as Aunt Augusta for the future.

CECILY: Thank you, Aunt Augusta.

LADY BRACKNELL: The marriage, I think, had better take place quite soon.

ALGERNON: Thank you, Aunt Augusta.

CECILY: Thank you, Aunt Augusta.

LADY BRACKNELL: To speak frankly, I am not in favour of long engagements. They give people the opportunity of finding out each other's character before marriage, which I think is never advisable.

JACK: I beg your pardon for interrupting you, Lady Bracknell, but this engagement is quite out of the question. I am Miss Cardew's guardian, and she cannot marry without my consent until she comes of age. That consent I absolutely decline to give.

LADY BRACKNELL: Upon what grounds may I ask? Algernon is an extremely, I may almost say an ostentatiously, eligible young man. He has nothing, but he looks everything. What more can one desire?

JACK: It pains me very much to have to speak frankly to you, Lady Bracknell, about your nephew, but the fact is that I do not approve at all of his moral character. I suspect him of being untruthful. (ALGERNON *and* CECILY *look at him in indignant amazement.*)

LADY BRACKNELL: Untruthful! My nephew Algernon? Impossible! He is an Oxonian.

JACK: I fear there can be no possible doubt about the matter. This afternoon during my temporary absence in London on an important question of romance, he obtained admission to my house by means of the false pretence of being my brother. Under an assumed name he drank, I've just been informed by my butler, an entire pint bottle of my Perrier-Jouet, Brut, '89; a wine I was specially reserving for myself. Continuing his disgraceful deception, he succeeded in the course of the afternoon in alienating the affections of my only ward. He subsequently stayed to tea, and devoured every single muffin. And what makes his conduct all the more heartless is, that he was perfectly well aware from the first that I have no brother, that I never had a brother, and that I don't intend to have a brother, not even of any kind. I distinctly told him so myself yesterday afternoon.

LADY BRACKNELL: Ahem! Mr. Worthing, after careful consideration I have decided entirely to overlook my nephew's conduct to you.

JACK: That is very generous of you, Lady Bracknell. My own decision, however, is unalterable. I decline to give my consent.

to interrupt to break into sb's speech or conversation

to come of age to become an adult

grounds here: reasons

ostentatious showing off unnecessarily

to approve of sth to think that sth is good

Oxonian sb who has attended the University of Oxford

temporary for a brief period

admission the right to enter

Perrier-Jouet, Brut, '89 an expensive sort of dry Champagne

to alienate to cause to become unfriendly or disloyal

subsequently afterwards

to devour to eat quickly, almost like an animal

unalterable unchangeable

Lady Bracknell: (*To* Cecily.) Come here, sweet child. (Cecily *goes over.*) How old are you, dear?

Cecily: Well, I am really only eighteen, but I always admit to twenty when I go to evening parties.

alteration change
calculating carefully planned in an uncaring manner
restraint control, limit
tutelage *Vormundschaft*

Lady Bracknell: You are perfectly right in making some slight alteration. Indeed, no woman should ever be quite accurate about her age. It looks so calculating ... (*In a meditative manner.*) Eighteen, but admitting to twenty at evening parties. Well, it will not be very long before you are of age and free from the restraints of tutelage. So I don't think your guardian's consent is, after all, a matter of any importance.

Jack: Pray excuse me, Lady Bracknell, for interrupting you again, but it is only fair to tell you that according to the terms of her grandfather's will Miss Cardew does not come legally of age till she is thirty-five.

instance in point a good example for this argument
accumulation process of growing into a large amount

Lady Bracknell: That does not seem to me to be a grave objection. Thirty-five is a very attractive age. London society is full of women of the very highest birth who have, of their own free choice, remained thirty-five for years. Lady Dumbleton is an instance in point. To my own knowledge she has been thirty-five ever since she arrived at the age of forty, which was many years ago now. I see no reason why our dear Cecily should not be even still more attractive at the age you mention than she is at present. There will be a large accumulation of property.

Cecily: Algy, could you wait for me till I was thirty-five?

Algernon: Of course I could, Cecily. You know I could.

punctual on time
punctuality

Cecily: Yes, I felt it instinctively, but I couldn't wait all that time. I hate waiting even five minutes for anybody. It always makes me rather cross. I am not punctual myself, I know, but I do like punctuality in others, and waiting, even to be married, is quite out of the question.

Algernon: Then what is to be done, Cecily?

Cecily: I don't know, Mr. Moncrieff.

Lady Bracknell: My dear Mr. Worthing, as Miss Cardew states positively that she cannot wait till she is thirty-five – a remark which I am bound to say seems to me to show a somewhat impatient nature – I would beg of you to reconsider your decision.

Jack: But my dear Lady Bracknell, the matter is entirely in your own hands. The moment you consent to my marriage with Gwendolen, I will most gladly allow your nephew to form an alliance with my ward.

Lady Bracknell: (*Rising and drawing herself up.*) You must be quite aware that what you propose is out of the question.

Jack: Then a passionate celibacy is all that any of us can look forward to.

Lady Bracknell: That is not the destiny I propose for Gwendolen. Algernon, of course, can choose for himself. (*Pulls out her watch.*) Come, dear, (Gwendolen *rises.*) we have already missed five, if not six, trains. To miss any more might expose us to comment on the platform.

(*Enter* Dr. Chasuble.)

Chasuble: Everything is quite ready for the christenings.

Lady Bracknell: The christenings, sir! Is not that somewhat premature?

Chasuble: (*Looking rather puzzled, and pointing to* Jack *and* Algernon.) Both these gentlemen have expressed a desire for immediate baptism.

Lady Bracknell: At their age? The idea is grotesque and irreligious! Algernon, I forbid you to be baptized. I will not hear of such excesses. Lord Bracknell would be highly displeased if he learned that that was the way in which you wasted your time and money.

Chasuble: Am I to understand then that there are to be no christenings at all this afternoon?

Jack: I don't think that, as things are now, it would be of much practical value to either of us, Dr. Chasuble.

Chasuble: I am grieved to hear such sentiments from you, Mr. Worthing. They savour of the heretical views of the Anabaptists, views that I have completely refuted in four of my unpublished sermons. However, as your present mood seems to be one peculiarly secular, I will return to the church at once. Indeed, I have just been informed by the pew-opener that for the last hour and a half Miss Prism has been waiting for me in the vestry.

Lady Bracknell: (*Starting.*) Miss Prism! Did I hear you mention a Miss Prism?

Chasuble: Yes, Lady Bracknell. I am on my way to join her.

Lady Bracknell: Pray allow me to detain you for a moment. This matter may prove to be one of vital importance to Lord Bracknell and myself. Is this Miss Prism a female of repellent aspect, remotely connected with education?

Chasuble: (*Somewhat indignantly.*) She is the most cultivated of ladies, and the very picture of respectability.

Lady Bracknell: It is obviously the same person. May I ask what position she holds in your household?

Chasuble: (*Severely.*) I am a celibate, madam.

Jack: (*Interposing.*) Miss Prism, Lady Bracknell, has been for

premature ahead of time

➔ Lord Bracknell never appears in person in the play. What picture of his life and marriage do we get?

grieved saddened

to savour of sth to appear to be like, to sound like

heretical against the official doctrine of the church

Anabaptists *Wiedertäufer*

to refute to argue against

secular worldly, non-religious

pew-opener sb who opens the rows of seats (pews) in a church

vestry a room or building attached to a church; *Sakristei*

to detain to keep back

repellent causing distaste or disgust

aspect appearance

celibate an unmarried person, esp. due to strong religious beliefs

to interpose to interrupt

the last three years Miss Cardew's esteemed governess and valued companion.

LADY BRACKNELL: In spite of what I hear of her, I must see her at once. Let her be sent for.

CHASUBLE: (*Looking off.*) She approaches; she is nigh.

(*Enter* MISS PRISM *hurriedly.*)

MISS PRISM: I was told you expected me in the vestry, dear Canon. I have been waiting for you there for an hour and three-quarters. (*Catches sight of* LADY BRACKNELL, *who has fixed her with a stony glare.* MISS PRISM *grows pale and quails. She looks anxiously round as if desirous to escape.*)

LADY BRACKNELL: (*In a severe, judicial voice.*) Prism! (MISS PRISM *bows her head in shame.*) Come here, Prism! (MISS PRISM *approaches in a humble manner.*) Prism! Where is that baby? (*General consternation. The* CANON *starts back in horror.* ALGERNON *and* JACK *pretend to be anxious to shield* CECILY *and* GWENDOLEN *from hearing the details of a terrible public scandal.*) Twenty-eight years ago, Prism, you left Lord Bracknell's house, Number 104, Upper Grosvenor Street, in charge of a perambulator that contained a baby of the male sex. You never returned. A few weeks later, through the elaborate investigations of the Metropolitan police, the perambulator was discovered at midnight, standing by itself in a remote corner of Bayswater. It contained the manuscript of a three-volume novel of more than usually revolting sentimentality. (MISS PRISM *starts in involuntary indignation.*) But the baby was not there! (*Everyone looks at* MISS PRISM.) Prism! Where is that baby? (*A pause.*)

MISS PRISM: Lady Bracknell, I admit with shame that I do not know. I only wish I did. The plain facts of the case are these. On the morning of the day you mention, a day that is for ever branded on my memory, I prepared as usual to take the baby out in its perambulator. I had also with me a somewhat old, but capacious hand-bag in which I had intended to place the manuscript of a work of fiction that I had written during my few unoccupied hours. In a moment of mental abstraction, for which I never can forgive myself, I deposited the manuscript in the basinette, and placed the baby in the hand-bag.

JACK: (*Who has been listening attentively.*) But where did you deposit the hand-bag?

MISS PRISM: Do not ask me, Mr. Worthing.

JACK: Miss Prism, this is a matter of no small importance to me. I insist on knowing where you deposited the hand-bag that contained that infant.

MISS PRISM: I left it in the cloak-room of one of the larger railway stations in London.

---

esteemed highly respected

nigh close, nearby

to quail to feel or show fear

desirous wanting to do sth

judicial here: like a judge

consternation shock, worry

to start here: to move suddenly

Metropolitan police The sector of Scotland Yard associated with the city of London.

perambulator pram; *Kinderwagen*

Bayswater a part of London in the City of Westminster

revolting disgusting

to brand to burn a mark onto sth

capacious large, able to hold many things

mental abstraction absence of mind

basinette (also: **bassinette**) here: sth to put a baby in

Jack: What railway station?

Miss Prism: (*Quite crushed.*) Victoria. The Brighton line. (*Sinks into a chair.*)

Jack: I must retire to my room for a moment. Gwendolen, wait here for me.

Gwendolen: If you are not too long, I will wait here for you all my life. (*Exit* Jack *in great excitement.*)

Chasuble: What do you think this means, Lady Bracknell?

Lady Bracknell: I dare not even suspect, Dr. Chasuble. I need hardly tell you that in families of high position strange coincidences are not supposed to occur. They are hardly considered the thing.

(*Noises heard overhead as if someone was throwing trunks about. Everyone looks up.*)

Cecily: Uncle Jack seems strangely agitated.

Chasuble: Your guardian has a very emotional nature.

Lady Bracknell: This noise is extremely unpleasant. It sounds as if he was having an argument. I dislike arguments of any kind. They are always vulgar, and often convincing.

Chasuble: (*Looking up.*) It has stopped now. (*The noise is redoubled.*)

Lady Bracknell: I wish he would arrive at some conclusion.

Gwendolen: This suspense is terrible. I hope it will last. (*Enter* Jack *with a hand-bag of black leather in his hand.*)

Jack: (*Rushing over to* Miss Prism.) Is this the hand-bag, Miss Prism? Examine it carefully before you speak. The happiness of more than one life depends on your answer.

Miss Prism: (*Calmly.*) It seems to be mine. Yes, here is the injury it received through the upsetting of a Gower Street omnibus in younger and happier days. Here is the stain on the lining caused by the explosion of a temperance beverage, an incident that occurred at Leamington. And here, on the lock, are my initials. I had forgotten that in an extravagant mood I had had them placed there. The bag is undoubtedly mine. I am delighted to have it so unexpectedly restored to me. It has been a great inconvenience being without it all these years.

Jack: (*In a pathetic voice.*) Miss Prism, more is restored to you than this hand-bag. I was the baby you placed in it.

Miss Prism: (*Amazed.*) You?

Jack: (*Embracing her.*) Yes … mother!

Miss Prism: (*Recoiling in indignant astonishment.*) Mr. Worthing! I am unmarried!

Jack: Unmarried! I do not deny that is a serious blow. But after all, who has the right to cast a stone against one who has suffered? Cannot repentance wipe out an act of folly? Why

coincidence sth that happens by chance
to occur to happen
trunk a large storage box

agitated nervous or troubled

to redouble to make or become much greater

injury damage
to injure
injurious

Gower Street in Camden, a part of London
stain a dirty mark that is difficult to remove
lining material covering the inside of sth; *Futter*
temperance beverage a drink that contains no alcohol
Leamington a place in the centre of England once famous for its spa *(Heilbad)*
initials first letters of one's name and surname
to restore to bring back
pathetic creating pity
to recoil to suddenly move backwards because of fear or disgust

to cast a stone biblical allusion to the Gospel of John 8:7 "Let him who is without sin cast the first stone"

repentance regret for past wrongdoing
to wipe out to make sth go away
folly foolishness

should there be one law for men, and another for women? Mother, I forgive you. (*Tries to embrace her again.*)

MISS PRISM: (*Still more indignant.*) Mr. Worthing, there is some error. (*Pointing to* LADY BRACKNELL.) There is the lady who can tell you who you really are.

inquisitive curious, wanting to find out
inquiry
to inquire

JACK: (*After a pause.*) Lady Bracknell, I hate to seem inquisitive, but would you kindly inform me who I am?

LADY BRACKNELL: I am afraid that the news I have to give you will not altogether please you. You are the son of my poor sister, Mrs. Moncrieff, and consequently Algernon's elder brother.

JACK: Algy's elder brother! Then I have a brother after all. I knew I had a brother! I always said I had a brother! Cecily, – how could you have ever doubted that I had a brother? (*Seizes hold of* ALGERNON.) Dr. Chasuble, my unfortunate brother. Miss Prism, my unfortunate brother. Gwendolen, my unfortunate brother. Algy, you young scoundrel, you will have to treat me with more respect in the future. You have never behaved to me like a brother in all your life.

ALGERNON: Well, not till to-day, old boy, I admit. I did my best, however, though I was out of practice.

(*Shakes hands.*)

GWENDOLEN: (*To* JACK.) My own! But what own are you? What is your Christian name, now that you have become some one else?

irrevocable unable to be changed

JACK: Good heavens! ... I had quite forgotten that point. Your decision on the subject of my name is irrevocable, I suppose?

GWENDOLEN: I never change, except in my affections.

CECILY: What a noble nature you have, Gwendolen!

JACK: Then the question had better be cleared up at once. Aunt Augusta, a moment. At the time when Miss Prism left me in the hand-bag, had I been christened already?

to lavish on to give sth in large quantities to sb
doting excessively loving or fond of sb

LADY BRACKNELL: Every luxury that money could buy, including christening, had been lavished on you by your fond and doting parents.

JACK: Then I was christened! That is settled. Now, what name was I given? Let me know the worst.

LADY BRACKNELL: Being the eldest son you were naturally christened after your father.

JACK: (*Irritably.*) Yes, but what was my father's Christian name?

to recall to remember
eccentric unconventional and slighty strange
indigestion pain or discomfort in the stomach

LADY BRACKNELL: (*Meditatively.*) I cannot at the present moment recall what the General's Christian name was. But I have no doubt he had one. He was eccentric, I admit. But only in later years. And that was the result of the Indian climate, and marriage, and indigestion, and other things of that kind.

JACK: Algy! Can't you recollect what our father's Christian name was?

ALGERNON: My dear boy, we were never even on speaking terms. He died before I was a year old.

JACK: His name would appear in the Army Lists of the period, I suppose, Aunt Augusta?

LADY BRACKNELL: The General was essentially a man of peace, except in his domestic life. But I have no doubt his name would appear in any military directory.

JACK: The Army Lists of the last forty years are here. These delightful records should have been my constant study. (*Rushes to bookcase and tears the books out.*) M. Generals ... Mallam, Maxbohm, Magley, what ghastly names they have – Markby, Migsby, Mobbs, Moncrieff! Lieutenant 1840, Captain, Lieutenant-Colonel, Colonel, General 1869, Christian names, Ernest John. (*Puts book very quietly down and speaks quite calmly.*) I always told you, Gwendolen, my name was Ernest, didn't I? Well, it is Ernest after all. I mean it naturally is Ernest.

LADY BRACKNELL: Yes, I remember now that the General was called Ernest, I knew I had some particular reason for disliking the name.

GWENDOLEN: Ernest! My own Ernest! I felt from the first that you could have no other name!

JACK: Gwendolen, it is a terrible thing for a man to find out suddenly that all his life he has been speaking nothing but the truth. Can you forgive me?

GWENDOLEN: I can. For I feel that you are sure to change.

JACK: My own one!

CHASUBLE: (*To* MISS PRISM.) Laetitia! (*Embraces her.*)

MISS PRISM: (*Enthusiastically.*) Frederick! At last!

ALGERNON: Cecily! (*Embraces her.*) At last!

JACK: Gwendolen! (*Embraces her.*) At last!

LADY BRACKNELL: My nephew, you seem to be displaying signs of triviality.

JACK: On the contrary, Aunt Augusta, I've now realised for the first time in my life the vital Importance of Being Earnest.

TABLEAU

CURTAIN

to recollect to remember

Army List list of all the officers in the army

domestic related to the home

directory book listing names and/or addresses

tableau a group of motionless people who represent a scene from a story

Con-Texts

Oscar Wilde – A Short Biography

Oscar Wilde is celebrated as one of the most brillant writers in the English language. Born on October 16, 1854 in Dublin, his full name was Oscar Fingal O'Flahertie Wills Wilde. A very bright student, especially of the classical languages Greek and Latin, he attended Trinity College in Dublin and Magdalen College at Oxford. In 1878, he left Oxford for London, where he quickly became well known, and later was to become one of the great writers of *fin de siècle* literature (a term referring to the end of the nineteenth century). Wilde was influenced not only by famous Victorian writers such as Algernon Swinburne and Walter Pater, but also by various French authors who stressed beautiful things more than moral considerations. In 1884, Wilde married Constance Lloyd; their first son Cyril was born in 1885 and their second son Vyvyan was born in 1886. Wilde wrote many poems, essays on various subjects and well-known stories such as *The Canterville Ghost, The Happy Prince, Lord Arthur Savile's Crime* and *The Selfish Giant.* He also wrote one novel that would become especially famous, *The Picture of Dorian Gray* (1891). Above and beyond this, Wilde was a successful playwright. In addition to *The Importance of Being Earnest* (1894), he wrote several other plays that are still regularly performed in many theatres. The most famous of these plays are *Lady Windermere's Fan* (1892), *A Woman of No Importance* (1893) and *An Ideal Husband* (1895), as well as one play written in French, *Salome* (1892).
Many of Wilde's witty sayings and remarks have become world famous. For Wilde, art was not meant to mirror reality, but was something autonomous. Wilde claimed that works of art can neither be moral nor immoral: "There is no such thing as a moral or an immoral book. Books are well written or badly written." His plays, in particular, contain many funny sentences that have contributed to his lasting popularity among theatre audiences. Despite the humour, Wilde's texts include serious criticisms of Victorian society that may not, however, have been obvious to contemporary audiences.

Unfortunately, Oscar Wilde's flamboyant lifestyle and his homosexual relationships provoked scandal in Victorian England. He was especially close to Lord Alfred Douglas, whose father did not approve of their friendship. This led to his imprisonment in 1895, because practising homosexuality was illegal at the time. Wilde spent two years in prison, having been sentenced to hard labour. After having served his term in prison, he moved to Paris, never to return to England or Ireland again. "The Ballad of Reading Gaol" is a poem based on his prison experiences and was published anonymously in 1898. His last great work of literature, however, was a letter to Douglas written in jail that was eventually published under the title *De Profundis* five years after Wilde's death. Prior to his death on November 30, 1900, Wilde lived for most of the time in Paris under the assumed name of "Sebastian Melmoth". On his death-bed, Wilde converted to Catholicism. (His last days in Paris are the subject of a fascinating novel by Peter Ackroyd, *The Last Testament of Oscar Wilde,* which brilliantly captures Wilde's character, thoughts and feelings.)
Wilde's fame as a writer has grown ever since. So much so that, one hundred years after his most important play, *The Importance of Being Earnest,* was staged in 1895, Oscar Wilde was even commemorated in Westminster Abbey's famous "Poet's Corner". Many of his plays – and even his life – have also since been turned into movies. Oscar Wilde's life and works have thus become an important part of our cultural memory.

The Historical Context

Queen Victoria

Oscar Wilde lived in the Victorian age, which is named after Queen Victoria, whose reign stretched from her accession to the throne in 1837 to her death 64 years later, in 1901. During this period, England became the wealthiest nation in the world and the British Empire expanded immensely: Victoria ruled over about 200 million people living outside Great Britain in such areas as India, North America and the South Pacific. Prime Minister Benjamin Disraeli even bestowed the title "Empress of India" on her to emphasize the power of the British empire.

Benjamin Disraeli

When Victoria was enthroned at the age of 18, the era of the railway had only just begun to replace the era of the stage coaches, but by the time of her death, the era of the automobile had already begun. The 19th century was thus a time of great transition and change. Hardly any epoch before had undergone similarly profound transformations in politics, society, religion and economy. Such changes were mainly due to the Industrial Revolution, which entailed both booms and depression. Urbanisation was growing and values and habits were changing along with it. The process of democratization was advancing slowly but surely as a result of various far-reaching political decisions, such as the First Reform Bill in 1832, which extended the vote to all men owning enough property.

Charles Dickens

Authors like Charles Dickens or Thomas Hardy highlighted many of the serious deficits of their time. Although the modernisation resulting from the Industrial Revolution had brought along with it an unimagined degree of mobility and flexibility, and with this also great intellectual progress, there were nevertheless severe downsides to this process: Three-quarters of the population lived in the quickly growing cities, which was leading to over-population. This was contributing in turn to the emergence of slums and to the brutal exploitation of workers. As a result, the slow-paced life in the country

Thomas Hardy

was rapidly being displaced for many people by a more mobile and active urban life. The ambiguities and contradictions of the Victorian era were many: At the same time people were encountering the fast development of technology, political reforms and progressive thinking, there was a strong emphasis on traditional Christian norms and values. One should note, however, that the rapid progress in science and technology was leading to increasing doubts about the truth of Christianity, which in turn was leading to feelings of deep insecurity among the elites of society. The impact of scientific theories such as Charles Darwin's theory of evolution was tremendous and was the source of many controversies.

Charles Darwin

A key concept for the Victorians was the family, which was regarded as the pillar of society and morality. Married women were idealised as *Angels in the House* – a phrase taken from a poem by Coventry Patmore. The task of these women, according to the dominant view of the time, was to care for their family and the household. Women were expected to behave properly so that they could be models of respectability. They were also expected to fulfil their duties towards their husbands and to uphold Christianity. Later, in the twentieth-century, Conservatives such as the British Prime Minister Margaret Thatcher (1979-1990) propagated a return to Victorian virtues such as self-help, hard work and frugality.

Victorians have often been described as narrow-minded and prudish. Critics have highlighted what they regard as the Victorians' hypocrisy. Rapid progress often entails the nostalgia for old values as a reaction against a deep-rooted sense of insecurity. In this world view, a good Christian is supposed to be serious about what he is doing. Oscar Wilde's *The Importance of Being Earnest* also portrays Victorian society as hypocritical, snobbish and narrow-minded. People are judged by their wealth and the social position of their families. The only way of escaping Victorian hypocrisy seems to be "bunburying" – if only this were not also a form of hypocrisy.

Social Life and Class in 19th Century Britain: The Aristocracy and the Lower Classes

Although Britain was a monarchy, ruled by Queen Victoria for most of the 19th century, it was also a parliamentary democracy. In 1832, the First Reform Act was the first of many later laws that would lead to a greater democratization of English society and politics. In 1884, the Third Reform Act, in particular, extended the vote to a much greater number of people. This meant that now about five million people could actually vote in elections. For the time being, women were still excluded from the vote, which led to the development of a women's suffrage movement that aimed to give the vote to women, too. Nevertheless, all of these developments did not change the dominance of the aristocracy in English politics and the society at large. In contrast to Germany, there were only very few socialist members of parliament at the time. Both political parties, the liberals and the conservatives, mostly agreed on keeping the power and wealth in the hands of the aristocracy and others with money, the so-called plutocracy.

The women's suffrage movement, London

The House of Lords, 1893

In the Victorian age, it was the aristocracy which firmly controlled the political system. The aristocracy managed to keep things like this until the beginning of the 20th century. In fact, in the 1880s, almost 400 MPs (= Members of Parliament) out of a total of 652, were members of the aristocracy. The aristocracy was composed of the nobility (which included those holding titles like Duke, Marquis, Earl and Viscount) and the gentry. Although the aristocracy suffered a decline in the course of the 19th century, as society changed greatly due in large part to the rise of the middle classes, the aristocracy nevertheless continued to set the standards of taste and lifestyle that many others wanted to follow. This included following aristocratic standards of education and building and refurnishing country houses.

A London slum

Uperclass lifestyle

The class system in England was never absolutely rigid. In fact, there was considerable upward and downward mobility. As the writer and historian A. N. Wilson once said: "The British class-system was always fluid, and anyone with luck, money or panache could always penetrate it". As only the eldest son of a member of the nobility inherited the title, many of the other family members had to work in what were called respectable professions. These, together with the landed gentry, came to constitute the upper middle class. There was, however, one feature of Victorian society that made moving between different social classes highly difficult: in the Victorian age the rich and the poor did not have much in common; their spheres of life were kept largely separate. Benjamin Disraeli spoke with good reason of the "two nations" – the rich and the poor – and these were more or less strictly separated from each other in Victorian England. The plight of the poor was all too real: millions of people did not own more than the clothes on their backs and their meager weekly earnings.

Comedy and Satire

Wilde's play *The Importance of Being Earnest* is, first and foremost, a comedy. In other words, it is a play with a happy ending. In fact, it is usually described as a *comedy of manners.* This means that it deals with the way certain kinds of people behave in circumstances that are depicted in a humorous way. The comedy of manners is a form of comedy that goes back to the late 17th century, the period of the Restoration after 1660. Essential elements of a comedy of manners are the following: it is set mostly in the city, its characters represent aristocratic ways of life, and the characters have to convey elegance and style, taste and good behaviour. The most important thing, however, is wit; that is, the ability to say clever and funny things.

A comedy of manners does not offer a very bitter view of society and human nature, or at least so it seems. Bitter criticism of mankind and society is more typically associated with the term 'satire'. Nevertheless, more serious criticism of social conditions and human nature may still be included in comedies of manner. This criticism is then satirical in nature: it satirizes the way of life of exactly the same sort of people who enjoyed going to the theatre and who were likely to also attend Wilde's plays – the fashionable society.

Satire has a long history, going back to at least the Romans, who first coined the term. What are the characteristic features of a satire? Satire is not so much a genre as a mode of writing. This means that novels and dramas as well as poetical works can all use the satirical mode in order to offer criticisms of human nature and society. Another Irish writer, Jonathan Swift, is famous for his satires.

Oscar Wilde uses satire in order to highlight what is ridiculous in Victorian society. His criticism does not aim at overthrowing this society but makes it possible for the audience to enjoy the absurdities of accepted social norms. By mixing social satire and absurd actions, melodrama and sentimentality, he manages to have the audience actually enjoy his criticism of their own social behaviour. In fact, there are good arguments claiming that Wilde's plays used both elements – satire and sentimentality – to address different sections of the theatre audience.

In conclusion, one can say that Wilde's play makes use of satirical elements but never develops a bitter or cynical view of human nature. Comedy always wins out, even though serious topics – like gender relations (especially marriage), the contrast between wealth and poverty, the absurdities of the British class system, superficiality and arrogance – are dealt with in the play.

Developing Skills

Drama: Useful Words and Phrases

• mood or feeling created by various factors such as scenery, lighting and sound effects, behaviour, tone of voice and diction of characters, etc.	**atmosphere**
• is reached when a conflict is at its highest point of tension; it often marks the turning-point of the action	**climax**
• literary work meant to be performed on stage • divided into acts and scenes	**drama/play**
• the audience understands implication and meaning of statement but character does not	**dramatic irony**
• can be happy/tragic/surprising	**ending**
• gives/provides information on the main characters, time and place of action • consists of/encompasses the first act/scenes • arouses reader's/audience's curiosity and interest	**exposition**
• tension begins to decrease • conflict is/cannot be solved	**falling action**
• any hints or clues that indicate what will happen later	**foreshadowing**
• use of words which are clearly the opposite of what one means • usually either to be amusing or to show annoyance	**irony**
• series of events causally linked • there may be a single line of action/a main plot and a sub plot	**plot**
• short for "stage properties" (e.g. pieces of furniture) used on stage	**props**

rising action
- develops the conflict
- leads to the climax
- tension/suspense is created (foreshadowing)

scene
- subdivision of play, usually marked by a change of place, entry or exit of character(s)
- traditionally: subdivision of an act

setting
- time and place of action
- social background/class
- scenery and properties (props) may be important to create a particular atmosphere or mood

stage directions
- notes added to the script of a play
- indicate a character's appearance, manner, style of delivery, performance, gestures and movements, details of location, scenery and effects

suspense
- state of curiosity, excitement and anxiety which the reader/audience experiences about the outcome of a situation

How to Write a Characterization

1. Mark/collect all the information that is given about a character

2. Introduce the character and the situation he/she is in. Refer to his/her social background/position/job/role in the family.

3. Start characterizing her/him directly, i.e. give age/describe outward appearance/consider what is said directly about the person (stage directions).

4. Refer to the traits of character that are revealed indirectly. Consider what a character does, how he/she reacts or behaves, what people think and feel, the mood they are in, how they respond to others.

5. Try to sum up if a character develops/changes in the course of events (complex/round) or if he/she does not change his/her attitude (flat character).

Characterization: Useful Words and Phrases

Mr/Mrs … is a man/woman in his/her (early/late) fifties/thirties/…
He/She … is presented/described as …
It is said that he/she looks/seems to be …
On the one hand, he/she is portrayed/depicted as a person who …
On the other hand, he/she …
It is characteristic of/typical of him/her that …
He/she is also characterized by his/her attitude towards …/reaction to …
which is revealed/underlined by his/her words/reactions/gestures/facial expressions …
He/she behaves arrogantly/pretends to be superior when …
He/she speaks in a low/loud voice/shouts at …
He/she shows emotions/feelings/that he/she is moved/nervous/excited irritated …
He/she seems to feel insecure/be convinced of himself/herself be in a bad/good mood
as/when he/she refers to/answers …
This idea is revealed when he/she says that "…" (l. …)
He/she is aware of the fact that …
His/her behaviour shows that he/she is curious/jealous/frightened/taken by surprise/self-confident/convinced that …/interested in …
His/her way of treating others … is harsh/friendly/gentle/arrogant/patronizing/contemptuous …
He/she creates the impression that he/she is a man/woman who …
An essential component of his/her character is …
The reader/audience may conclude from his/her behaviour that …
During the evening/play/in the course of action, he/she undergoes a development/remains essentially unchanged
The character changes his/her attitude towards …
He/she is a flat/complex (round) character/an individual and not just a mere social type
One can easily identify with …/you feel pity/sympathize with/dislike him/her because …

➊ Are there any additional words and phrases?

Analysing a Dramatic Text (a Play)

Basic vocabulary and expressions

Tragedy	Comedy
according to Aristotle: **unified** action (unity of action, time and place), deals with the **downfall** of a person caused by a **flaw**; the events **arouse pity** and fear in the audience	according to Aristotle: comedy depicts human beings as worse than they are in reality; it concerns the **domestic lives** of **ordinary people**
hero/heroine becomes involved in a situation which is **inescapable**	often, comedy **ridicules antisocial** behaviour; frequently, **coarse** language is used and sexual themes are frankly dealt with
the tragedy concerns great events and **noble** characters	Classical comedy has **stock characters** who represent **social types**, with little individualization
the events **inevitably** lead to a **catastrophic conclusion/disaster**	the events lead to a **resolution** and **happy ending**

The structure

The action develops in a number of stages:

1. exposition	The characters, themes, setting, etc. are introduced.
2. rising action	A conflict is developed.
3. climax	The conflict reaches its highest point.
4. turning point	There is a change in the conflict or suspense.
5. falling action	Suspense is reduced.
6. denouement	A resolution of the conflict is achieved (happy ending or catastrophic conclusion)

Elements of analysis

Preliminaries
- act/scene/line
- stage/stage directions or instructions
- setting
- atmosphere (gloomy, tense, relaxed, troubled, mysterious, full of impending doom, cheerlessness/desolation, harmony/understanding, discord, hostility, despondency)

The author evokes an atmosphere of ...
The playwright creates/establishes a mood of ...
The setting contributes to an atmosphere of ...
The overriding mood is ...
The dominant atmosphere is ...

Characters
- hero/heroine
- protagonist/antagonist
- main, central/minor character/ figure
- flat character/round character

The hero leaves the stage.
The author shows the hero's motives/feelings.
The main character is the mouthpiece of the author.
The character oscillates between ...
In this scene, the main characters are on stage.

Action
- the starting point
- sobplots/main plot
- conflict, complication, crisis
- plot
- flashback
- falling action/rising action

The action is set in a big city.
The intrigue begins to develop.
The progress of the plot is slowed down.
The function of the scene is the acceleration of the action.

Dialogue/Monologue
- interlocutor
- answer/reply/react
- soliloquy
- address sb/respond to sb
- reaction/response

The subject/function of the dialogue/monologue is ...
In his soliloquy, the protagonist reveals his motives.
In this monologue, the heroine addresses the audience.